The Canadian Indian

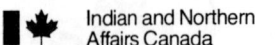 Indian and Northern Affairs Canada   Affaires indiennes et du Nord Canada

Published under the authority of the
Hon. Bill McKnight, P.C., M.P.,
Minister of Indian Affairs and
Northern Development,
Ottawa, 1986.

QS-6026-000-EE-A1
Catalogue No. R32-76 1986E
ISBN 0-662-14747-2

Cette publication peut aussi être obtenue
en francais sous le titre:
Les Indiens du Canada

© Minister of Supply and Services Canada

Cover photo: E.S. Curtis/Public Archives Canada

Title page photo: E.S. Curtis/Public Archives Canada

Table of Contents

5	**General Introduction**

6	**The People and their Cultures**
6	Tribal Origins
6	The Peoples' Languages
8	The Culture Areas: A Survey
9	*Woodland Indians*
14	*Indians of Southeastern Ontario*
21	*Plains Indians*
27	*Indians of the Plateau*
33	*Pacific Coast Indians*
42	*Indians of the Mackenzie and Yukon River Basins*

49	**The Newcomers**
49	First Encounters
50	Religious Missions
51	The Ravages of Disease
51	Intertribal Conflict
52	French versus English
53	Indian Rights
53	The Western Fur Trade
54	Experiments in Acculturation
56	The Robinson Treaties
56	An Act for "Gradual Civilization"
56	The Metis Resistance
57	The Major Treaties
59	The Northwest Rebellion of 1885
59	Treaties for the Northern Reaches
60	The First "Indian Act"

86	**The Age of Resurgence**
86	The Joint Committee Hearings (1946-48)
87	The 1951 Indian Act
87	The 1969 White Paper
88	Indian Control of Indian Education
89	The James Bay and Northern Quebec Agreement
91	Indian Rights Confirmed
91	Native Claims
92	Comprehensive Claims
94	Specific Claims
94	Economic Development
95	Historic Breakthroughs of the 1980s
96	The Special Committee on Indian Self-government
97	The Elimination of Sex Discrimination
99	Directory of Indian and Related Organizations
101	Selected Reading

General Introduction

Canada's first people crossed the Bering Strait from Asia well over 25 000 years ago. By the time Europeans discovered the New World, the Indian population had developed a host of cultures, societies and linguistic groups.

These Indian cultures varied as widely as the terrain of Canada itself. In the wide prairie interior, small groups of families co-operated in hunting the migratory buffalo which provided the meat and skins necessary for their survival. These people designed shelters to suit their nomadic existence. The tipi — a conical pole structure covered with skins — was portable, easily erected, warm, well ventilated and sound enough to weather strong winds.

The Pacific Coast Indians, on the other hand, evolved a very different culture. The bounty of the sea — salmon, shellfish and the great whale — made possible the establishment of permanent villages and leisure time to carve from cedar and stone magnificent art objects now housed in museums throughout the world.

Equally distinct and unique were the cultures of the nomadic Woodland people, the tribes of the British Columbia interior plateau, the Iroquoian farmers of southern Ontario and the hunters of the northern barren lands.

All these cultures had in common a deep spiritual relationship with the land and the life forms it supported. Indian religion saw human beings as participants in a world of inter-related spiritual forms. The people maintained a reverence for the spirits of animals, trees and rocks.

With the arrival of European newcomers, this delicate balance of life forms was disrupted. The introduction of firearms and diseases previously unknown to Indian people brought widespread devastation. For many decades, the Indian population declined and the very existence of their unique cultures was threatened.

By the 1940s, Indian leaders once again asserted themselves. They sought to overcome the government control which had tainted traditional Indian cultures.

Through decades of dedication and persistence, Indian people have succeeded in making the government and the general public aware that they were once free, self-sustaining nations. Today, in seeking their own forms of self-government, they want to assume their rightful place in Canadian society. At the same time, they want to maintain the rich diversity of their traditional cultures which evolved over thousands of years before European contact.

The People and their Cultures

Tribal Origins

Most anthropologists agree that the North American Indian originated in Asia, migrating over the Bering Sea from Siberia.

There is much more doubt about exactly when these migrations started. Ample evidence exists to show that man was present in the New World as early as 10 000 B.C. More recently, however, the discovery of crude, chipped stone implements has led some historians to set the date back farther still to 40 000 B.C.

The first inhabitants of a largely glacier-covered North America were hunters. They hunted big game animals like the giant sloth and the mammoth, both of which were much larger than any land mammal of the 20th century.

The weapons hunters used were wooden lances with sharp stone heads, made by painstakingly chipping pieces from flint rock. Prehistorians speculate that hunters made their attacks at very close range, probably when the animal was mired in a bog.

The Big Game Hunting Culture flourished in Canada's plains and eastern woodlands until about 8000 B.C. In Canada's far west there developed a similar ancient hunting and fishing culture known as Old Cordilleran.

When the glaciers began to melt, the gradually warming climate changed the face of the land and dramatically affected the wildlife. The mammoth soon became extinct. In the forests surrounding the lakes left by retreating glaciers, the people hunted deer, bear, elk and smaller game.

The culture that originated in this moist, forested region has come to be known as Boreal Archaic. Lasting until about 6000 B.C., it was marked by the use of various woodworking tools, including axes, gouges and adzes. With these, the Boreal Archaic Indians were able to make dugout canoes.

By 1000 B.C., the Early Woodland Culture had developed in eastern North America. During this period, the population became more stable and individual cultures began to crystallize. New features such as pottery and ceremonial burials were gradually incorporated into the cultures of Canada's prehistoric tribes.

The Peoples' Languages

Communication was essential within each of these new stabilized cultures. Through language, the people of a particular culture group could share their experiences and world view. Over thousands of years, the different Indian tribes occupying Canada developed distinct languages, each of which reflected a unique lifestyle.

Anthropologists and linguists have classified the languages traditionally spoken by Canadian Indian tribes into various language families. Each language family is made up of individual but related languages derived from a parent language. This classification of the various Indian languages into different language families is the result of long study and careful comparison of sounds and individual words and meanings from language to language.

Ten Canadian Indian language families are recognized today: Algonkian, Iroquoian, Siouan, Athapaskan, Kootenayan, Salishan, Wakashan, Tsimshian, Haida and Tlingit. Together, these 10 families comprise more than 50 individual languages which evolved in Canada.

In the past, as today, Indians belonging to the same language family did not necessarily share the same culture. The Blackfoot of the plains and the Micmac of the Maritimes, for example, are both classified as belonging to the Algonkian family but their cultures have traditionally been radically different.

Native Linguistic Families

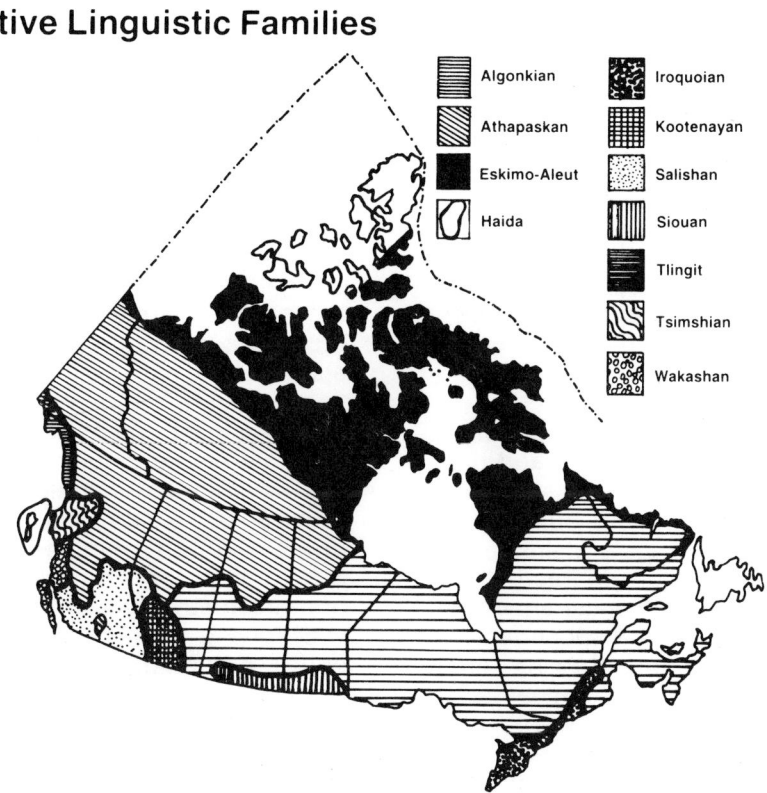

Conversely, Indians who shared the same cultural background did not necessarily belong to the same language family. This was particularly true on the Pacific coast where people of the Salishan, Wakashan, Tsimshian and Haida language families shared a common culture.

Because the various tribes inhabiting the Pacific coast at the turn of the century traded extensively among themselves, they found it necessary to adopt a common trade language. The solution was a simplified form of Chinook, an indigenous language originating in Washington state.

In addition to the four language families of the Pacific coast, there were three others — Kootenayan, Athapaskan and Tlingit — in the interior plateau of British Columbia. This means that seven of Canada's Indian language families were found west of the Alberta-British Columbia border. Linguists have suggested that this great diversity of separate languages was due to the geography of British Columbia itself. The inland mountains, the deeply indented fjords of the shoreline and the scattered coastal islands all tended to isolate the different tribal groups.

Like the Indians of the Pacific coast, the Plains Indians shared a common culture and spoke languages belonging to three different families — Siouan, Algonkian and Athapaskan. So mobile were the skilled horsemen of the plains that there was frequent interaction between the various tribes. To communicate, they developed an elaborate gesture language consisting of about 800 signs.

The Culture Areas: A Survey

A culture area has been designated as a geographical area occupied by a number of tribes whose cultures resembled each other significantly. These tribes may have spoken different languages and belonged to different language families.

Six such Indian culture areas have generally been recognized by anthropologists. In each of these, the geographical environment played a large part in shaping the culture itself.

Before Europeans arrived, the Indians of Canada were able to satisfy all their material and spiritual needs by using the resources of the natural world that surrounded them. The environment and the life forms it supported provided materials for clothing, dwellings and food.

Canada's easternmost culture area was that of the Woodland Indians. The environment in which they lived was dense boreal forest, bordering in the north on a tundra-like land. Moose, deer, bear, beaver and caribou provided tribes from this area with food and clothing. Adding variety to their diets were fresh-water fish and fowl of the inland rivers and lakes, and the abundant shellfish and cod found along the maritime coast. The Woodland Indians' environment was one of extreme temperatures with long cold winters and short, hot summers. Given the harsh climate, even the cultivation of root crops was a difficult undertaking.

By contrast, Canada's southernmost culture area was one of the country's most fertile regions. The Iroquoian Indians lived in a lush, rolling land watered by rivers and streams. To the north, it was bordered by forests inhabited by deer, beaver and bear. The area's outstanding characteristic, however, was its temperate climate. With an average growing season of 140 days, the Iroquoian tribes had ample time to plant and cultivate crops of corn, beans and squash.

The culture area of the Plains Indians consisted of seemingly endless grasslands, occasionally broken by ridges of hills and running streams. Despite its apparent desert-like character, the plains abounded with wildlife. Herds of antelope thrived there, as did North America's largest land mammal, the buffalo.

The culture area of the Plateau Indians marked the transition between Canada's prairies and the Pacific coast. This area was a land of contrasts ranging from semi-desert conditions in the south to high mountains and dense forest in the north. Salmon teemed in the headwaters of the Fraser, Thompson and Columbia rivers. Land mammals such as mountain goat and sheep, moose, elk, caribou, deer and bear inhabited this area.

Indians of the Pacific Coast culture area obtained their food supply by harvesting salmon, shellfish and whales from the sea. The land they inhabited had a mild climate and heavy rainfall. Dense forests of gigantic red cedar bordered coastal villages.

The Indians of the Mackenzie and Yukon River basins endured a much harsher way of life. Their culture area consisted of sombre forests, barren lands and the swampy terrain known as muskeg. Migratory animals such as caribou and moose were more scattered and scarcer than in the eastern woodlands. The long, severe winters challenged those small communities who lived in this area.

Woodland Indians

Principal Tribes

There were eight principal tribes of Woodland Indians, all of whom spoke languages belonging to the Algonkian family. The now extinct Beothuk lived in Newfoundland, while the Micmac occupied Nova Scotia, northeastern New Brunswick, Gaspé in Quebec, and Prince Edward Island. Southwestern New Brunswick and the neighbouring part of Quebec were the home of the Malecite.

The Montagnais and Naskapi lived in what is now Quebec and Labrador. The Montagnais occupied the heavily wooded area along the north shore of the St. Lawrence as far east as Sept-Iles. The tundra-like lands of the Naskapi extended far into northeastern Quebec.

The Ojibway (sometimes called the Chippewa) occupied a large territory encompassing all the northern shores of Lake Huron and Lake Superior from Georgian Bay to the edge of the prairies, and to the height of the land north where the rivers begin to flow towards Hudson Bay. The Algonkin lived in the Ottawa valley.

Flanking the Ojibway on the north and west, the Cree also occupied an immense area. They lived on the southern perimeter of Hudson Bay, living as far north as Churchill. Their territory was bounded on the east by Lake Mistassini and extended all the way west to the prairie frontier.

Social Organization

For the most part, each of the Woodland tribes was divided into numerous bands that possessed their own hunting territory and were politically independent of each other. Consisting of a number of related families, bands seldom exceeded 400 people. Each band had a leader, usually someone who had won the position through a display of courage, strength of character, or skill in hunting. In theory, every individual in the band was equal, so that the leader enjoyed few, if any, special privileges.

Some tribes (notably the Micmac and the Ojibway) were divided into several clans, each with its own symbol. The Micmac adorned their clothing with their clan symbol, and painted it on their canoes, snowshoes and other possessions. The Ojibway were comprised of more than 20 clans, each of which was named after the creature thought to have founded it. The moose, lynx, bear, wolf and crane were some of the animals deemed to have founded their respective clans.

Woodland Indian hunters and trappers had an intimate knowledge of the habitats and seasonal movements of animals, fish and fowl. Bands had to follow their migratory quarry, travelling from hunting ground to hunting ground as soon as the yield began to slacken. The density of game was not the same in all regions. In northern Ontario and Quebec, the animals were so scattered that even the best hunters sometimes faced starvation.

To provide for times of hardship, during the summer months every band carefully dried all the meat, fish and berries it could safely store away.

Modes of Transport

Because mobility was essential for the Woodland Indians' survival, their technology was adapted to the environment and the manufacture of light-weight, easily portable goods.

The birch bark canoe was a light, durable, streamlined vessel built to navigate the numerous rivers and lakes. It could accommodate the needs of a hunting party and, as with the Ojibway, a family group harvesting wild rice in the shallows of lakes throughout the Lake of the Woods area. To make a canoe, bark sheets were stitched together and subsequently fastened to a wooden frame using *watup* — white spruce root that had been split, peeled and soaked. The seams of the vessel were thoroughly waterproofed with a coating of heated spruce gum and grease. Easily carried on portages, the canoe could be readily repaired from materials available in the forest.

During winter, when the river system froze, canoes were cached. It was then that toboggans were used for transporting possessions. Snowshoes were used by winter travellers. The Cree preferred the "bearpaw", a broad oval-shaped shoe. The Micmac used two varieties, both with square toes. One was large, for use on fluffy snow, while the lighter type was ideal for snow with a frozen crust.

Another important transportation device was the tumpline — a broad leather strap shaped like a sling. The wide loop of the sling was passed over the packer's forehead, while its two ends secured the pack itself so that it rested comfortably on a carrier's back.

Moss-lined bags were used to carry babies. Woodland Indian mothers strapped these bags securely to wooden cradles in such a way that the baby stood upright, its feet resting on a little shelf at the bottom.

Dwellings

All Woodland tribes had homes that were either portable or easily erected from materials at hand. Their *wigwams* were essentially a framework of poles covered with bark, woven rush mats or caribou skin. A hole cut in the roof ensured ventilation.

Most tribes preferred the conical wigwam that could be erected in an hour. Both the Ojibway and the Cree, however, used dome-shaped wigwams occasionally.

Inside the wigwam, belongings were stowed around the edges, just under the poles. All the space around the central hearth was strewn with fir boughs to provide insulation against the damp ground. The boughs were covered with rush mats and fur bedding.

In winter, to increase warmth, the eastern Cree often cleared away the snow on the floor inside the shelter and hollowed out the soil to a depth of 10 centimetres so that the living area was below the frost line.

Woodland Indians transported only the coverings of their dwellings, as they could always count on finding the necessary poles at the next site. Consequently, they were able to break camp and move within minutes.

The Use of Bark

The Woodland Indians had a host of uses for durable, light-weight tree bark, especially that of the birch. They boiled food in water-filled bark vessels by dropping heated stones into the water. Bark was used for all kinds of containers, including boxes, baskets, trays, dishes and spoons. Women sometimes created artistic designs on birch bark by making precise indentations with their teeth.

Birch bark could also serve as a temporary raincoat. Messages and directions drawn on bark were used to guide travellers. Through a rolled cone made from birch bark, an expert hunter could call any moose within earshot.

Hunting and Trapping Techniques

While winter brought hardship, it did offer advantages. In deep snow, for example, a moose's tracks were plainly visible, making it easier for hunters to stalk the animal. Moving quickly on their light-weight snowshoes, hunters could soon overtake an animal sunk to its belly in deep, soft snow.

Hunting methods consisted mainly of stalking animals. Spears and bows and arrows were used to fell the prey. Traps and snares were also used to capture animals. One of the commonest traps was the log deadfall; when the animal tried to take the bait, it triggered a heavy log which fell on its back, killing it outright. The snare, used to trap both large and small animals, was essentially a noose that caught the creature by the neck or leg. Snares were made either of animal sinew or *babiche*, a rawhide thong.

Extensive fences were sometimes built along woodland trails frequented by moose or deer. Snares were hidden in strategically placed gaps in the fence. The Naskapi hunted caribou with snares suspended along both natural and artificial trails where animals had to pass. When their antlers became entangled, they were easily killed with spears or arrows.

With the exception of the Cree, nearly all Woodland Indians engaged in fishing. This was often done using *weirs* — fences or barriers built in a stream so as to trap fish, yet allow the water to flow. These weirs were usually made of a lattice-work and brush.

Clothing

Most clothing was made of moose, deer and caribou skin. Garments worn by Woodland Indians were tailored tunics and leggings, moccasins and a breech or loin cloth for the men. Women dressed in much the same way, converting the tunic into a flowing gown by extending it to the knees or ankles. In winter, robes of fur, usually woven of strips of rabbit skin, added extra warmth. Caps and mittens were made from the pelts of muskrat, beaver and other furbearing animals. Possibly borrowing from the coastal Inuit, the Naskapi fitted their tailored coats with hoods for winter use.

The Ojibway coloured their clothing with red, yellow, blue and green dyes derived from flowers, roots and berries. Intricately patterned porcupine-quill and moose-hair embroidery adorned hunters' gauntlets and women's moccasins.

Women processed the animal skins, dehairing and flensing each hide, and then soaking it and stretching it taut. Smoke tanning was the process often used to preserve the hide. Working with a stone knife to cut the skins, a bodkin to punch the holes and a bone needle, women sewed the clothing with sinew taken from the back or legs of caribou, moose or deer. Making babiche (a remarkably strong leather cord) was another of the women's tasks. Babiche was used to secure loads, as a resilient webbing in snowshoes and as lacing for a cradleboard.

Other essential chores done by the women in each community included making the fish nets, gathering firewood and cooking.

Spiritual Beliefs and Ceremonies

Many of the religious beliefs of the Woodland Indians were integrated with their hunting practices. The bear, for example, was treated with particular respect. A hunter would talk or sing to the bear before killing it, assuring the animal that its death was required only because the hunter and his family needed food. As a mark of respect, the skulls of bears and beavers were carefully cleaned and then placed high on a pole or in a tree where dogs could not defile them.

Certain practices were believed to reinforce the relationship between hunters and animal spirits. The Naskapi, for example, held a special ritual feast called *Mokoshan* at which they ate the bone marrow of caribou. Hunters might also carry charms to help in hunting. Beaks, claws, a weasel's skull or, as with the eastern Cree, the dried decorated head of the first goose of the year, were some of these charms.

During adolescence young men embarked on a vision quest and sought a lifetime guardian spirit who would help them in hunting and other activities.

People also paid close attention to visions and dreams: to dream of sunbeams striking the ground was thought to be particularly auspicious for the hunter.

The *djasakid*, a special kind of shaman who conducted the "shaking tent" ceremony, helped locate lost people and objects and predicted where game could be found. After dark, the djasakid would be bound hand and foot in a small, circular lodge. When he sang, the lodge would sway and shake. He would then send the spirits in search of caribou and moose and report in an unfamiliar voice what they had seen.

The regular shaman generally treated illnesses by placing a tube on the patient's body and sucking out the disease-causing object. He and many of the women were also adept at herbal remedies.

The Ojibway had an elite group of medicine men known as the *Medewiwin*, or Grand Medicine Society. This group held elaborate healing ceremonies. Both male and female candidates underwent a purification ritual, entering a sweat lodge where the scented vapours of an intensely hot, herbal sauna cleansed their bodies and spirits. The society recognized four grades of membership, and even the lowest level required a long period of instruction in gathering herbs, diagnosing illnesses and curing the sick.

By singing, drumming and participating in the ritual use of tobacco, the Woodland Indians believed it was possible to build up one's power or *manitou*, the pervasive spirit in human beings and nature.

The drum was the most important of the Woodland Indians' musical instruments. Both the tambourine and double-headed type of drum were used. There was also a small, barrel-shaped water drum which made an echoing note capable of carrying a long distance.

Indians of Southeastern Ontario

Principal Tribes

There were nine principal Iroquoian tribes, all of whom spoke languages belonging to the Iroquoian language family. The Huron lived between Lake Simcoe and Georgian Bay. To the south and west were their allies, the Tobacco Nation (also called the Petun).

Further south still on the Niagara Peninsula lived the Neutral. The villages of the Erie Indian tribe bordered on the southern shoreline of the lake which has their name.

South of Lake Ontario and extending to the upper St. Lawrence River was the land of the Iroquois, a confederacy of five tribes: the Mohawk, the Oneida, the Onondaga, the Cayuga and the Seneca. In 1722 the Iroquois confederacy was joined by a sixth tribe — the Tuscarora.

Social Organization

Superb farmers, the Iroquoian tribes annually harvested food crops that more than met their needs. This abundance of food had far-reaching consequences for their culture. It made possible a stable community life in stark contrast to that of the nomadic Woodland Indians. It also allowed the Iroquoians the stability and leisure required to devise complex systems of government based on democratic principles.

The Huron government system, for example, was so arranged that not even the smallest unit was ever called upon to surrender its rights. This system grew out of the family structure: eight *exogamous matrilineal clans* that deeply influenced marriage patterns, personal identity and ceremonial life. (An exogamous clan is one whose members can marry only outside the clan; matrilineal means tracing descent through the female line). Totemic animals such as the bear, beaver, deer and wolf identified each clan. Because these same clans were common to all Huron villages, they provided important, permanent links within the Huron confederacy.

Each clan segment had two chiefs: the civil chief and the war chief. The civil chief was chosen for qualities like intelligence, oratorical powers, generosity and performance as a warrior. To ensure that he would be able to represent his clan effectively, he had to have the support of other Huron headmen. The civil headman managed all the internal affairs of his clan segment and could be removed from office only by his own clansmen. Nor could he be compelled against his will to accept any decision made by other headmen. A village council composed of all the headmen in the village met daily.

Huron government was essentially a three-tier political system, consisting of the village councils, tribal councils and the confederacy council. As well as strengthening ties of friendship within the confederacy, the annual meetings of the confederacy council co-ordinated dealings with enemy tribes. Decision making was carried on by consensus, discussions often going late into the night until a satisfactory agreement was reached.

Like the Huron, the Iroquois were divided into matrilineal exogamous clans, each with its identifying totem animal. Despite this potential for unity, there was a time when the tribes of the Iroquois warred among themselves.

According to tradition, a prophet named *Dekanawideh* approached all the feuding tribes in the land of the Iroquois, proclaiming the Great Peace. Out of his efforts emerged a powerful council of all the chiefs of the five Iroquois tribes. These 50 men drafted the laws of the confederacy. While the exact date of the founding of the Iroquois League is uncertain, it is thought to be sometime in the 15th century.

All the chiefs who constituted the council of the league had to agree to be of "one heart, one mind, one law". Any decision making amongst them required unanimous agreement. They met whenever necessary to arbitrate on intertribal problems or decide on war or peace with outside tribes.

The league itself was symbolized by a *longhouse* (the traditional Iroquois dwelling place), with the Mohawk guarding the east door, the Onondaga tending the hearth, and the Seneca guarding the west door. Flanking the Onondaga at the central hearth were the Cayuga on the south wall and the Oneida on the north.

When one of the league's 50 chiefs died, the clan matron chose a successor in consultation with other women of her clan. If the person chosen proved unsatisfactory, his chief's name could be revoked by the clan mother. The Iroquois called this process "dehorning" the chief because the deer antlers that symbolized his office were taken away.

The Three Sisters

The Iroquoian peoples raised corn, beans and squash. So closely associated were these three plants that the Iroquois called them "The Three Sisters". The three plants were physically linked, corn and beans being planted in the same mound, so that the corn stalks would support the climbing beans; the squash, planted at the same time, grew on the flat ground between the mounds, their broad leaves discouraging weeds.

The Huron had costumed dancers who represented the three plants and participated in rites dedicated to the fertility of the earth and the productivity of the crops.

Despite the abundant meat, fish and fowl available in the wild, the Iroquoian tribes subsisted primarily on their own crops. It has been estimated that the average daily diet of the Huron was 65 per cent corn (about 550 grams a day); 15 per cent beans, squash and sunflower seeds; 10 per cent fish; 5 per cent meat such as deer or rabbit; and 5 per cent wild forest products like berries, nuts, maple sugar and leafy vegetables.

In total, the Huron grew 15 varieties of corn, 60 different types of beans and six kinds of squash.

Farming Methods

It was the men who cleared the land, chopping down trees and cutting the brush. Planting, tending and harvesting the crops were done by the women.

Using moose antler or deer scapula hoes, the women hoed the earth into mounds. Then they used a digging stick to make a hole for the seeds several centimetres deep in each mound.

The seeds themselves were selected on the basis of size, taste and colour and whether or not the plant matured rapidly. Corn kernels were usually germinated in a bed of moist bark.

For at least six months of the year, the women and children lived and worked in the fields, planting in May, weeding and chasing away predators through June, July and August, and harvesting and drying the plants for storage in September. Squash was preserved in underground caches lined with bark and covered with earth; the corn and beans were stored in large bark chests inside the houses.

Because the Iroquoians had no knowledge of fertilizers, the soil of any given field would become exhausted after three or four years. New fields would be used up in turn and after about 10 years, a community would have to relocate.

Villages

Compared with the nomadic Woodland Indians, the Iroquoian tribes had relatively permanent villages. Potential village sites had to meet certain standards, including availability of well-drained, arable soil, a good supply of drinking water, proximity to a forest for necessary firewood and construction materials, and a locale easily defended against attack from hostile tribes. Hilltop sites were favoured for this reason, and the various tribes also took advantage of natural obstacles (such as swamps) for averting possible attacks.

Iroquoian settlements varied in size from hamlets of 50 people to villages of 1 000 or more. Mohawk villages tended to be smaller, those of the Huron and the Seneca were the largest. The corn fields around the villages often covered immense areas. In 1677, for example, the Onondaga reportedly had corn fields stretching three kilometres on either side of their hilltop village.

Fortifications

For the Iroquoians, warfare was the means by which young men gained prestige. Blood revenge was the primary motive for warrior raids. Frequently one tribe or confederacy of tribes attacked another to avenge the deaths of comrades killed in previous battles.

Consequently, all the larger Iroquoian villages, and those on the frontier of enemy territory, were strongly fortified. In the event of attack, people in the smaller villages fled to regional strongholds or hid in the forest.

The Huron built elaborate palisades to help fend off the Iroquois, their traditional enemy. These palisades consisted of as many as three tightly set rows of upright posts. Varying in height from five to 11 metres, these poles were often securely interlaced with branches and bark.

Where palisades were sufficiently wide, galleries were built inside from which the defending forces could shoot arrows, drop rocks on those attempting to scale the walls or throw water to extinguish fires set by the enemy.

Dwellings

The most conspicuous feature of the Iroquoian village was the longhouse, itself a symbol of the large family that lived within. Each longhouse belonged to a matrilineage headed by a powerful matron. It was she who oversaw day-to-day affairs within the house. The household usually included her husband, her unmarried sons, her daughters and their husbands and children. Normally, after he married, a man moved into the longhouse where his wife lived.

House construction began with two parallel lines of poles which were then bent toward each other and combined with others to form the roof. Once the inverted U-frame was completed, it was covered with slabs of bark — elm bark among the Iroquois, and cedar bark among the Huron. A line of smoke holes on the roof could be widened in summer and narrowed in winter simply by shifting the bark on the roof.

The size of the longhouse varied according to the number of family members. Usually, a longhouse was about 10 metres wide, 10 metres high and 25 metres long. A row of hearths ran down the central passageway. Each hearth was shared by two small families living opposite each other. Sleeping platforms were set along the walls just high enough to avoid the damp ground, but not so high as to catch the smoke.

Arranged in clusters of related families, the longhouses were built sufficiently far apart to hinder the spread of fire.

The construction of an Iroquoian settlement was no small matter. For a palisaded village of 1 000 people in 36 longhouses, about 20 000 large poles were required. A town crier would sometimes go through the village calling for assistance when a new house was being built. For the most part, however, the construction work was done by the male members of the extended family using the house.

Division of Labour

The tasks of Iroquoian men and women were clearly defined. In addition to taking total responsibility for the crops, women gathered firewood, prepared skins and made clothing. Household utensils such as pottery and baskets and mats of reeds, bark and corn husks were made by community women. They were also responsible for cooking, and often prepared a thin soup made of corn meal to which pieces of fish, meat or squash were added. They ground the corn in a hollowed-out tree trunk, using a wooden pestle about two metres long.

Men's contribution to the economy included the construction of dwellings and palisades. They also partook in hunting and fishing expeditions. In addition to the deadfall traps and twist-up snares used by most Iroquoian tribes, blowguns and darts for hunting birds and small game were used by the Iroquois themselves. For the Huron, deer hunting was a largely co-operative activity. As many as several hundred men would drive the animals into a river or a specially constructed enclosure where they were easily slaughtered.

The Huron built canoes which, like those of the Woodland Indians, were covered with bark. The Iroquois, on the other hand, were essentially landsmen. Being excellent runners, they could cover extremely long distances in a remarkably short time.

Men also manufactured stone tools and weapons and made spoons, bowls, warrior clubs and suits of armour from wood.

Buckskin clothing was relatively simple in design, although sometimes brightly decorated with paint and porcupine-quill embroidery. Women wore a skirt and, on occasion, a jacket. Men wore a loin cloth, adding leggings and shirts when the weather was cool. Both men and women used moccasins. The Iroquois sometimes made their footwear from braided corn husks.

Trading Missions

During the summer, Iroquoian men embarked on trading missions to exchange goods both with their allies and neighbouring northern Woodland tribes such as the Algonkin. The Neutral, for example, bartered with the Algonkin for prime animal pelts and porcupine quills. In return, they provided the Algonkian-speakers with corn, tobacco, fishing tackle and wampum (white and purple beads made from shells and much valued as a medium of exchange).

In addition to direct trading with their allies and the Woodland Indians, the Huron monopolized all the Tobacco Nation's trading activities, acting as middlemen and profiting from the barter of corn and tobacco.

Warfare

With the exception of the Neutral and Tobacco nations, who preferred a peaceful existence, Iroquoian tribes engaged in raiding parties from late spring until early autumn.

Responding to requests from families who had lost members to the enemy, Huron war chiefs organized military forays, going from village to village, explaining their plans and encouraging young men to join them.

For distance fighting the principal weapons were bows and arrows. Ball-headed clubs were used for close combat. Some Iroquoian tribes had armour made of pieces of wood laced together with cord, or sheets of wickerwork covered with rawhide. Most warriors carried a small bag of roasted corn meal which could last for several weeks. This corn was supplemented by fish or meat obtained along the way.

The capture of prisoners enhanced a warrior's reputation. Although very often subjected to cruel tortures in the captor's village, a substantial number of prisoners were adopted into the enemy's tribe. In general, a prisoner would be adopted by a family who had lost a warrior in battle.

Spiritual Beliefs and Ceremonies

The Huron believed that everything, including fabricated things, had a soul and was immortal. Souls having the power to influence human beings were called *oki*. Because it controlled the seasons and other natural phenomena, the oki of the sky was considered the most powerful.

Huron adolescents also undertook a vision quest, seeking out the guardian spirit who would reveal the personal war chant they were to sing in times of danger.

The most important shamans were those who healed the sick. There were two kinds: the *ocata*, who diagnosed and suggested treatment for all sorts of illnesses, and the *aretsan*, who specialized in removing spells cast by witches.

Both the Huron and the Iroquois had curing societies. The Iroquois False Face Curing Society was, however, perhaps the most famous. Carved wooden masks used in the rite were believed to possess spiritual force and depicted a hierarchy of mythical beings. Grimacing and contorted, each wooden mask conferred special curative powers on the society member who wore it.

For the Iroquoians in general, the winter months were the time for socializing and for festivals. The *Ononharoia* — the main Huron winter festival — was a soul-curing ritual. It was celebrated at least once a year in every large village, either because many people were ill or depressed or because some important person was ill. During this three-day celebration, people broke into houses, upset furniture and shattered pots. Those who were sick then went about the village seeking out objects that had appeared in their dreams. If they got what they were looking for, it signified that their troubles were over.

The most important of all Huron festivals was the Feast of the Dead. Held only once every decade, the feast usually involved several satellite communities.

During the 10-day feast, the community's dead were removed from their individual graves and reinterred in a common ossuary. Eight of the 10 days were spent in careful preparation of the corpses, whose flesh was stripped and then burned.

Presents brought by family mourners were collected and redistributed by a village headman. The Feast of the Dead was, for the Huron, an act of reverence which also promoted goodwill among neighbouring communities.

The Iroquois annually held six to eight festivals associated with the cultivation of the soil and the ripening of fruits and berries. There was a seven-day festival when corn was planted, another when it was green, and a third when it was harvested. The outstanding event in the Iroquois ceremonial year was the Mid-Winter Festival which extended over a week, the final three days being reserved for games. During the festival, tobacco was burned and the Creator was asked for success in the coming agricultural year.

Plains Indians

Principal Tribes

There were eight principal tribes of Plains Indians in Canada. Of these, the Blackfoot, Blood, Piegan, Gros Ventre and Plains Cree spoke languages belonging to the Algonkian language family. The Assiniboine and Sioux spoke languages belonging to the Siouan family. The Sarcee spoke an Athapaskan language.

The Blackfoot (or *Siksika*) had territory east of the Rocky Mountains in the high plains where Edmonton and Calgary are now. The Blackfoot, together with the Blood and the Piegan, formed a powerful alliance.

The Blood lived to the southwest of the Blackfoot, close to the foothills of the Rockies. The Piegan lived south of the Blood, in the regions now known as Lethbridge and Medicine Hat.

Before 1800, the Gros Ventre lived east of the Piegan. The country of the Plains Cree stretched across the northern fringe of the plains, south of the Churchill River to the eastern edge of Blackfoot territory.

The Assiniboine occupied all the area south of the Plains Cree, from the eastern plains to Blackfoot country. The Sioux (or *Dakota*) were a large confederacy scattered over the American plains and the Canadian west. Today, several hundred Sioux live on reserves in Manitoba and Saskatchewan. They are the descendants of refugees who came to Canada under the leadership of Sitting Bull after the defeat of the American cavalry at Little Bighorn in 1876.

The Sarcee, who came from the north by way of Lesser Slave Lake, lived along the upper part of the Athabasca River, northwest of the Blackfoot.

Social Organization

All the prairie tribes were composed of individual bands, each of which had a chief and usually several councillors. During the summer, bands assembled and either selected a tribal chief or simply acknowledged the authority of a particular chief who had outstanding influence. At these gatherings, the bands pitched their tipis in a circle with the council tent in the centre.

The Plains Indians had military societies which performed various functions, including policing, regulating life in camp and on the march, and organizing the defences.

The military societies of the Blackfoot, known collectively as the *aiinikiks*, or All-Comrades, had one or two leaders who sat on the tribal council when the bands united during the summer. Membership in the All-Comrades was by purchase only. Promotion in the various societies was basically age-graded. Every four years a man could sell his membership to a younger man and purchase that of an older man in the next appropriate society. Every grade, however, had to include at least four elderly men amongst its members so that wise counsel and experience were available at each stage.

Modes of Transport

The image of the Plains Indian on horseback has stirred the imagination of people throughout the world. But, in fact, the Plains Indians' adaptation to the horse was a relatively recent development. It was only about 1730 that the Blackfoot first acquired horses.

Before the introduction of the horse, the Plains Indians wandered on foot, following the buffalo migrations. So dependent were they on the buffalo, that they moved camp even more frequently than did the nomadic Woodland Indians.

In the days of wandering, the principal means of transporting goods and household possessions was the dog and travois. The travois consisted of two long poles hitched to the dog's sides. A webbed frame for holding baggage was then fastened between the poles behind the dog. A large dog could carry as much as 35 kilograms on a travois; each family usually owned several animals.

The recency of the horse in Plains Indian culture is reflected in the names given to the animal. These names were based on the horse's dog-related traits. The Blackfoot called the horse "elk-dog" because of its great size. For the Sarcee, the horse was "seven-dogs" because it was able to carry or pull much more weight than any dog.

Plains Indians adapted readily to the horse and were skilled riders. They developed technical terms for different types of horses, including those used for hunting buffalo or pulling the travois. Within 100 years following its introduction, the horse was therefore an intrinsic part of Plains Indian culture, whether in hunting, warfare, travel or transportation of goods.

Dwellings

Like the Indians of the eastern woodlands, the Plains Indians needed portable dwellings. When relocating, they transported both the dwelling coverings and the poles used to support them. The poles for their tipis were usually made from long, slender pine trees, and were much valued since replacements were not readily available in the prairies.

Perfectly straight and smoothly peeled of bark, 12 to 20 poles were used to form the tipi's conical structure. The foundation poles, on which all the others rested, might be either three or four in number. The Blackfoot, Blood, Piegan and Sarcee used the four-pole foundation, while the Assiniboine, Cree and Gros Ventre used three poles.

Once the foundation poles were firmly positioned in the ground, the other poles were laid in the crotches formed at the top. The last pole to go up was the one that went in the back of the tipi. The tipi cover was tied to it so that they both went up together. The cover was then brought around the two sides to the front and fastened above the doorway with pegs. Before the introduction of the horse, a tipi cover consisted of six to eight buffalo hides stitched together. Once the horse made herds more accessible, however, the average tipi cover was about 12 skins. To prevent a draft and give interior ventilation, there was often an inner wall of skins about two metres high, fastened to the poles on the inside.

The bottom of the tipi was secured either by pegs driven into the ground or by several sizeable stones. At the top of the tipi were two flaps, each attached to an outside pole which could be adjusted to regulate the draft or ventilate the tent.

The tipi was not a perfectly symmetrical cone but rather slightly tilted. It was steeper at the back, and the smoke hole extended down the gently sloping front. Besides improving ventilation, this tilt enlarged the space at the back of the tipi where most activity took place. The tilt also helped brace the shorter face of the cone against the wind.

The hearth fire was built just behind the centre of the tipi. The place of honour, reserved for the head of the family, was located opposite the door flap. Furniture consisted of light-weight triangular backrests, made of willow and bound together with cord. Fur bedding served as couches during the day. Bags of food, tools, weapons and garments were hung from the pole framework.

It was the women who made, erected and owned the tipis. Although the men were primarily hunters and warriors, they also made weapons, shields, tools, drums and pipes.

Other duties performed by women included butchering, drying and preparing meat and processing skins from which they made clothing and leather bags.

Food Preparation

A single buffalo provided a great amount of meat, the bulls averaging 700 kilograms and the cows 450 kilograms.

Eaten fresh, the meat was roasted on a spit or boiled in a skin bag with hot stones, a process that also produced a rich, nutritious soup.

Equally common was the dried meat known as *jerky*. Meat to be dried was taken from the animal's lean parts and cut into thin slices. These were slit until they resembled coarse netting and were then hung on racks to dry in the sun. Once thoroughly dried, jerky could be stored for a long time in rawhide bags called *parfleches*.

Pemmican was prepared by the women who pounded dried meat into a powder which was then mixed with hot, melted buffalo fat. The resulting product was a high-protein food used by the travelling hunter or warrior. It was easily carried in small leather bags. Packed away in tightly sewn skin bags, pemmican would remain edible for years.

The Tanning Process

Plains Indian women were experts in tanning skins. Tanning was a long and tiring process considered so important that a woman was judged largely on the quality and quantity of skins she tanned.

Even the simplest process — making the hard, stiff rawhide for moccasin soles and parfleches — was arduous and exhausting. Staked flat on the ground with the skin-side down, the hide was first thoroughly scraped to remove all shreds of fat and meat. Next, it was reversed and all the hair scraped off until the skin was clean and soft. It was then left to dry and harden.

To produce a soft skin, this same process was followed, and the hard rawhide was thoroughly rubbed with a mixture of animal brains, fat and liver. This was done by hand, sometimes using a smooth stone. After drying in the sun, the hide was soaked in water, rolled into a bundle and left to cure. It then had to be stretched and scraped again on both sides. The final step entailed many hours of rubbing and kneading until the skin was soft and pliable. The total process took about a week.

Clothing

For the most part, clothing was made of light skins such as buffalo, antelope, elk or deer. Heavy buffalo skins with the shaggy hair left on were fashioned into robes to be worn in cold weather.

Men usually wore a breech cloth held up by a belt. Attached to this were soft leather thongs supporting long leggings. A knife sheath and small bag for face paint might also hang from the belt. Moccasins and a skin shirt in cool weather completed the outfit.

Women's shirts reached just below the knee, and their leggings tied just above. In general, the sides of their shirts were laced together.

The magnificent, full feather headdress so often associated with the North American Indian was originally worn only by a few important leaders of the Sioux. Members of other warrior societies, however, had different headdresses which were sometimes adorned with buffalo horns. Blackfoot society members wore headdresses made from the white winter skins of the weasel. White eagle feathers with sharp, black tips were also much admired, and, when worn in the hair, symbolized acts of bravery.

Many men wore face paint regularly. Red was a favourite colour. The Sarcee often painted the whole upper portion of their faces with ochre and vermilion.

The Buffalo Hunt

The Plains Indians encountered by European newcomers between 1830 and 1880 had a highly developed hunting culture. The buffalo was the prime object of their hunt and posed a formidable challenge. In addition to its imposing size, the buffalo had keen senses of smell and hearing.

Before the advent of the horse, tribes like the Blackfoot, Assiniboine and Plains Cree devised effective hunting techniques which were a match for this powerful prey. Along either side of traditional buffalo migration routes hunters would arrange clusters of brush, branches and stones so that these barriers converged at a chosen location on the plain. These V-shaped alignments served to direct the buffalo into a corral at the end of the funnel where the animals were slaughtered by the hunters. The main weapon used was the bow and arrow, made from either ash or willow.

Another type of drive was known as the buffalo jump. For this hunting technique, the hunters took advantage of locations where the open terrain suddenly gave way to steep cliffs. By stampeding entire herds over a precipice, the hunters could obtain large quantities of meat from a single expedition.

In the "surround" technique, hunters would band together on their horses and encircle a group of animals. While most hunters remained on the perimeter carefully aiming their arrows, others entered into the thick of the milling buffalo to make their kill. As the animals were slaughtered, the horsemen reduced the size of the circle.

Communal hunts took place in June, July and August when the buffalo were fat, their meat prime and their hides easily dressed. The hunters themselves shared the tasks of butchering and skinning the animals, and the carcasses were divided according to the needs of each family. A special allotment was made for the sick and aged of the band.

The Plains Indians put the buffalo to a host of other uses. Its horns served as spoons and drinking cups and its bones as scrapers. Sinew was used as thread. The shaggy hair was plaited into halters. Hooves were boiled and rendered into glue. When wood was scarce, dried buffalo excrement was a good source of fuel, producing relatively little smoke.

Warfare

The Plains Indians conducted three types of raids: small expeditions to steal horses from other tribes, game-like "coups" for scoring points for bravery against the enemy without necessarily killing or injuring, and major war expeditions to seek or protect territory.

Before the coming of European traders, the weapons used in intertribal warfare were the bow and arrow, spears, clubs and knives. While some men wore protective jackets of several layers of leather, shields were much more popular. Shields were round and made from the heavy chest skin of an old bull buffalo. Decorated with eagle feathers symbolizing bravery, the shields were often painted with sacred designs and images from the warrior's dreams.

Large scale warfare was well organized. Smoke signalling and surprise attack were tactics frequently used. A technique similar to the buffalo surround was also used, with the warriors on horseback circling the enemy, shooting as they drew closer.

Towards the end of his life, an elderly Plains Indian would often paint on a piece of buffalo skin a series of pictographs to record his war deeds for all time.

Spiritual Beliefs and Ceremonies

The various Plains Indian tribes had similar religious beliefs. Great spirits worshipped were the Sun, the Thunderbird and Napiwa, the Old Man of the Dawn. These the Sioux called *wakan tanka* — the greatest sacred ones.

The adolescent vision-quest was an intense spiritual experience for the warrior of the plains. A guardian spirit would give a young man his own war song or dance, or indicate what amulets he should wear to give him power. Many of the symbols painted on tipis and war shields with porous bone brushes originated in the owner's vision-quest.

Religious "medicine bundles" carried by tribesmen consisted of magical amulets (feathers, birds' beaks or oddly shaped stones) wrapped in skin. Every object had a unique significance and called for a special song when its owner exposed it to the light. The medicine bundle gave its owners prestige and was thought to bring them wealth and good fortune.

Peace pipe ceremonies also played a part in the Plains Indian religion. Often carved from catlinite, a smooth red stone, the pipes were used in a ritual which involved blowing smoke toward each of the four cardinal directions, then skyward and finally to earth.

Ritual purification was sought through the intense heat and drenching steam of the sweat lodge. New participants often chewed on a piece of sage, the same herb being sprinkled on the lodge floor, to prevent themselves from passing out in the almost overwhelming heat.

In addition to military societies, there were numerous dancing societies which had social and religious functions. Dances generally reflected the culture's emphasis on hunting and warfare and were usually performed at the tribe's summer gathering. One dance, with five men in a line, was specifically for warriors who had never run from the enemy. Another dance paid homage to men noted for their liberal sharing of meat after a hunt.

One of the most dramatic of the dance ceremonies was the annual Blackfoot sun dance. The construction of the sun dance lodge began with the erection of a central pole hung with offerings to the Great Spirit. This was surrounded with a circle of 10 more poles and the whole structure covered with leafy branches. The classic sun dance involved only a few men who fasted, prayed and danced from the circle wall to the central pole and back. Traditionally, the end of the dance entailed some self-torture with sharp skewers being forced through the skin of the dancer's back and chest. Such self-torture was, however, more popular among United States tribes like the Sioux.

Indians of the Plateau

Principal Tribes

Six principal tribes occupied the diversified plateau area of interior British Columbia.

The Interior Salish was the largest of these tribes and consisted of five groups belonging to the Salishan language family. The Lillooet Indians lived in the Lillooet River Valley. South and west of them were the Thompson Indians, who occupied the Fraser River Valley from Yale to Lillooet. The most northerly and largest of the groups was the Shuswap, who controlled the Fraser River from Lillooet to Alexandria and east to the Rocky Mountains. The most southerly was the Okanagan, who lived in the Okanagan River Valley. To their east around the Arrow Lakes and the upper Columbia River were the Lake Indians.

Until about 1750, the Kootenay tribe lived east of the Rockies on the prairies. Driven westward over the mountains by the Blackfoot, they came to occupy the southeastern corner of British Columbia. They belonged to the Kootenayan language family.

Occupying the headwaters of the Chilcotin River and the Anahim Lake district were the Chilcotin, a tribe belonging to the Athapaskan language family. To their north were the Carrier, who belonged to the same language family. They lived in the large area comprising the valleys of the upper Fraser, Blackwater, Nechako and Bulkley rivers.

The third tribe of Athapaskan speakers was the Tahltan, who lived north of the Carrier and controlled the lands of the drainage basin of the upper Stikine River. North of the Tahltan, in the valley of the upper Lewes River, lived the Tagish, who belonged to the Tlingit language family.

The Plateau culture area was essentially a great valley between the Rocky Mountain and coastal ranges and featured several different environments. The southernmost part was semi-desert, with cactus, sagebrush and rattlesnakes. The central region's rushing rivers and waterfalls ran thick with salmon in spring. To the north, near the Cascade Range, lay a land abundant in moose, deer and caribou.

Despite the variety of local environments, the Indians of the British Columbia interior all used similar methods for hunting and fishing and for cooking and preserving their food. Their house designs, however, varied from region to region. There were also marked differences in the social organization of the various tribes.

Social Organization

Several of the Plateau tribes were influenced by their neighbours, who were the Indians of the Pacific coast. These influences were intensified by well-established trade activities.

In exchange for skins and moccasins, for example, the Carrier Indians obtained cedar boxes and Chilkat blankets woven by the Alaskan Chilkat Indians from the Bella Coola and Tsimshian tribes of the coast. As a result of these transactions, they assimilated the stratified social system of the Pacific Coast tribes and began restructuring their population into nobles, commoners and slaves. Intermarriage with the Tsimshian of the Skeena River helped strengthen this process. Both the Chilcotin and the Tahltan adopted similar social systems: the Chilcotin through their fur trade with the coastal Bella Coola and the Tahltan by way of trade activities with the Alaskan Tlingit of the Pacific coast.

Of the Interior Salish groups, the Lillooet were the chief intermediary for coastal trade. They shipped dried berries, tanned skins and mountain goat wool to the coast. In return, they received seashells and dugout canoes, adopting at the same time the Pacific Coast belief in supernatural clan ancestors. Other social influences from coastal communities included winter dances in which participants wore animal masks, and the founding of secret religious societies.

Despite their close trading ties with the coast, the Interior Salish groups did not adopt the class system. Rather, each small band of several related families recognized the authority of a hereditary chief. An informal council of elders assisted him in his decision making. Hunting territory belonged to the band as a whole, although some families laid claim to specific fishing stations and berry-picking grounds.

The Kootenay followed a similar system, each band having a hereditary leader supported by a council of elders. A special chief was elected both for their annual buffalo hunt across the foothills of the Rockies and for the times the Kootenay were at war — particularly with the Blackfoot.

Fishing Techniques

Salmon was a primary food source for the Indians of the plateau area. Even the Tahltan hunters of the north assembled each spring at the fishing places to await the arrival of the first salmon. The Chilcotin regularly bought salmon from the Shuswap. The Kootenay, however returned each year to their original prairie homeland to hunt the buffalo.

During the summer months countless salmon swam upstream to spawn in the headwaters of the Pacific-bound rivers. The Plateau Indians developed several techniques to benefit from this annual migration. The Carrier, for example, constructed weirs in the shallows of swift waters to block and trap schools of fish. Another method took advantage of the salmon's habit of leaping up over waterfalls. Basketry screens with curled bottom edges were firmly set at the top of the waterfall so that the jumping fish were caught fast when they fell backward.

Many of the Plateau fishermen used dip nets, positioning themselves on a rocky ledge just above a swiftly flowing current. The twine for the nets was made from Indian hemp, nettle fibres or the inner bark of the willow. Another popular device was the two-pronged spear, each prong having its own detachable harpoon head.

Of the thousands of salmon caught each year, a very small proportion was eaten fresh. The remainder of the annual catch was cleaned, smoked over a slow fire and stored for winter in underground pits lined with birch bark.

Salmon were also boiled by the hot stone method. Oily fish heads were added to the broth, and when the mixture cooled the oil was skimmed off the top. This salmon oil, combined with dried, powdered fish and saskatoon berries, made a nutritious, long-lasting fish pemmican.

The most commonly used cooking vessels were watertight baskets made of tightly wound split roots of spruce and cedar. The baskets fashioned by the Thompson and Lillooet women featured geometric motifs and were colourfully decorated with natural dyes.

Hunting Methods

The principal weapons for hunting were the bow and arrow, spears and knives. In the southern area of the plateau, bows were made of yew wood or of juniper. In the north, willow or spruce was used. A wrapping of deer sinew or rattlesnake skin was often added to strengthen the bow. The bow-string itself was deer sinew.

Arrows were made of either cedar or saskatoon wood. Lillooet hunters bit the wood of their arrows to break the grain and so prevent warping.

Many tribes used nets to catch waterfowl. The Carrier would stretch a net between two canoes and drive flocks of grebe (a bird resembling the loon) into it. To trap ducks, the Kootenay strung nets at the tops of poles high above the birds' feeding grounds.

In addition to deadfall traps and snares, the Plateau Indians made widespread use of pitfalls. A narrow, steep-sided pit would be dug in a deer trail, then carefully camouflaged with a top layer of twigs and leaves. The pits were so constructed that once the animal fell in, it was unable to free itself.

Hunters who were stalking deer would sometimes disguise themselves with a deerskin coat and a hat made of a deer's head. Before setting out, Lillooet hunters rubbed themselves with tree twigs to help remove their human scent.

Gathering

Wild vegetable foods — chiefly roots and berries — formed an important part of the diet of the Plateau Indians, particularly the Interior Salish.

Among the most important roots gathered was camas, a wild lily with a large bulb. There were two types of camas — an edible one with a blue flower and poisonous one with a white flower. To avoid any possible confusion, bulbs were dug up only when the lily was in bloom. Other edible roots included the wild onion, or *lillooet*, the inner portion of the skunk cabbage and water parsnip roots, which could be eaten fresh. The primary tool for root digging was a curved piece of yew with a handle fashioned from a mountain sheep horn. The Lillooet also used sticks made of deer antler.

Because cooking roots was a task requiring considerable expertise, it was undertaken only by the older women in the band. First, a shallow pit in the ground was filled with red-hot stones. As soon as the ground surrounding the pit got intensely hot, the women raked out the stones and laid down a layer of camas bulbs. Next came a layer of leaves, then more hot stones. Finally, a heat-insulating layer of earth and skins was applied. Left to cook overnight, the bulbs broke down into a black, pulpy mass that would keep for months after it had cooled and dried. Using the same method, the

Interior Salish cooked a black tree moss found hanging on Douglas fir trees.

The women also had a special method of preserving the thousands of berries they picked during the early autumn. Saskatoon berries, salmon berries, raspberries and blueberries were dried in the sun on racks of cedar covered with large leaves. The addition of berry juice helped solidify the resulting berry cakes.

Another popular vegetable food was the inner bark of the evergreen and poplar. Collected in the spring when the sap was rising, the soft juicy bark had a sweet taste a little like oranges. The bark was removed in long slivers with a special scraper of thin bone or antler. Hung to dry, these slivers would keep for several months.

Modes of Transport

Water travel was minimal in the plateau area. There were several reasons for this, one being the nature of the rivers themselves. Both the Fraser and Thompson rivers were so full of rapids that the Interior Salish did most of their travel by foot. Nevertheless, the Thompson Indians did have three types of canoe; birch bark, cedar dugouts and skin-covered wooden frames.

Another factor restricting travel was food preference. The Carrier, for example, were so dependent on fish that they felt no need to hunt in the winter, subsisting on their stores of dried salmon. They therefore had neither snowshoes nor toboggans.

Amongst the northern Tahltan, on the other hand, winter hunting was a necessity. But because wood was scarce in their region, nearly all travel was by foot. They did, however, use toboggans made from the leg skins of the moose. Many tribes, the Kootenay in particular, used dogs to pack heavy loads when travelling.

Dwellings

Nowhere were the differences between the Plateau tribes more apparent than in the homes they built for themselves. These ranged from the subterranean dwellings of the Interior Salish to the Kootenay's buffalo hide tipis.

The subterranean dwellings of the Interior Salish were unlike the dwellings of any other Indian tribe in the country. Construction began with digging a round hole in well-drained gravelly soil, generally close to a river. Water, fish and a means of transport were thus all accessible. These pits were usually about two metres deep and from six to 12 metres wide.

Once the pit floor was well covered with spruce boughs, a conical framework of poles was erected. An opening approximately 1.25 metres square was left at the top to serve as both smoke-hole and doorway. The framework was then insulated with spruce boughs, more poles and the earth that had been removed from the pit.

The house was accessible by steps carved in a sturdy, slanting log, the top of which protruded through the opening. The houses were large enough for several families to have separate sleeping areas and to gather around the centrally-positioned cooking fire for meals and other domestic activities. Dried food was cached outside the dwelling in boxes raised on posts or in deep, bark-lined pits.

During summer the Interior Salish moved above ground into oblong or conical lodges covered with rush mats.

Farther to the north the Carrier built rectangular winter houses of cedar slabs. Gabled roofs covered with spruce bark made these homes distinctive. The roofs slanted right down to the ground on each side, doing away with the need for upright walls.

The homes of the Tahltan were double lean-tos made of poles covered with spruce bark. Often long enough to house several families, these homes looked like two open tents facing each other.

Clothing

There was a distinct uniformity in the kind of clothing the various Plateau tribes wore. Except among the Kootenay who preferred moose hide, garments were usually made of deerskin.

Men wore a buckskin shirt, breech cloth, leggings and moccasins. The women wore shorter leggings and a longer version of the shirt. In winter, both men and women donned robes of woven rabbit skins or groundhog fur. Ornamental touches included fringes and lines of red ochre occasionally applied along the seams of clothes. The Interior Salish also wore decorative blankets of mountain goat's wool.

Spiritual Beliefs and Ceremonies

Among the Interior Salish, adolescent vision-seekers would sometimes paint rocks with abstract designs depicting tasks they undertook while in seclusion. As part of their training for adult responsibilities, young women were expected to spend many hours at monotonous, physically demanding tasks — digging ditches or plucking needles from fir trees.

The Tahltan had similar practices. Girls underwent a two-year period of seclusion in a separate hut where they received intensive training for womanhood. Young Tahltan men underwent frequent fasting in pursuit of visions. Once their animal guardian spirit appeared, they would seek out and kill its real counterpart in the wild and preserve the animal's skin as an amulet.

The Carrier sought the aid of supernatural beings by practising various rituals. They believed that men with spiritual gifts could gain closer contact with the supernatural world through fasting and dreaming in

Dear Reader,

At Indian and Northern Affairs Canada, we want to ensure that communications with our audiences are as effective as possible.

Please tell us what you think of this publication by answering the brief questionnaire on the other side of this card. Detach the response section and mail. No postage is required.

Appropriate measures will be taken to protect the confidentiality of the respondent.

Thank you for your co-operation and quick response.

Cher lecteur,

Aux Affaires indiennes et du Nord Canada, nous tenons à rester en contact avec notre public.

Pour nous dire ce que vous pensez de cette publication, veuillez remplir le questionnaire qui se trouve a l'endos de cette carte, détachez la carte-réponse et postez-la. N'ajoutez pas de timbre, nous nous chargeons de l'affranchissement.

Des mesures appropriées assurent le caractère confidentiel des renseignements fournis par les répondants.

Nous vous remercions de nous avoir accordé ces quelques minutes de votre temps.

Business Reply Mail
No postage stamp necessary if mailed in Canada

Department of Indian Affairs and Northern Development Communications Branch
Room 658
Les Terrasses de la Chaudière
Ottawa, Ontario
K1A 0H4

Correspondance-réponse d'affaires
Se poste sans timbre au Canada

Le port sera payé par

Ministère des Affaires indiennes et du Nord canadien
Direction générale des communications
Pièce 658
Les Terrasses de la Chaudière
Ottawa (Ontario)

Postes Canada / Canada Post 5013

TB/CT-REG. B26004-1

Canada

Indian and Northern Affairs Canada / Affaires indiennes et du Nord Canada

PUBLICATION USER SATISFACTION QUESTIONNAIRE
QUESTIONNAIRE RELATIF À LA SATISFACTION DU CLIENT

1 Please answer the questions by completing the response card on the right.
Veuillez répondre aux questions sur la carte-réponse à droite.

Which of the groups listed best describes you?
Auquel de ces groupes vous identifiez-vous le mieux?

2 What percentage of the publication did you read?
Quel pourcentage de la publication avez-vous lu?

3 How satisfied were you with the clarity, relevance and informational value of the material contained in this publication? Please rate your level of satisfaction.
Que pensez-vous de la clarté et de la pertinence des articles et de l'information contenue dans cette publication? Indiquez votre degré de satisfaction.

4 Any additional comments or explanations?
Avez-vous des observations ou des explications à ajouter?

60-7 (3-85) 7530-21-036-8286

Tear Along Perforation and Mail – Détachez et postez

Name of Publication – Titre de publication

The Canadian Indian
QS-6026-000-EE-A1

1 EDUCATION – ÉDUCATION
- ☐ Teacher / Enseignant
- ☐ Elementary / Primaire
- ☐ Indian School Teacher / Enseignant (école indienne)
- ☐ High School / Secondaire
- ☐ University / College / Université / collège
- ☐ Student / Étudiant

GOVERNMENT – GOUVERNEMENT
- ☐ Indian and Northern Affairs / HQ / Affaires Indiennes et du Nord / A.C.
- ☐ Other Fed. Dept. / Autre min. féd
- ☐ Prov. Gov't / Gouv. prov
- ☐ Other Gov't / Autres ordres de gouv
- ☐ Territorial Gov't / Gouv. territorial
- ☐ Indian and Northern Affairs / Region / Affaires Indiennes et du Nord / Région
- ☐ Legislators / Législateurs

OTHER – AUTRES
- ☐ Native Groups / Groupes autochtones
- ☐ Libraries / Bibliothèques
- ☐ Other / Autre
- ☐ Media / Média
- ☐ Scientists / Researcher / Sciences / Recherches
- ☐ Business / Affaires
- ☐ Associations
- ☐ General Public / Grand public

2 ☐ 0% ☐ 25% ☐ 50% ☐ 75% ☐ 100%

3

Attribute / Critères	Very Satisfied / Très satisfait	Satisfied / Satisfait	Neither Satisfied or Dissatisfied / Ni satisfait ni insatisfait	Dissatisfied / Insatisfait	Very Dissatisfied / Très insatisfait
Clarity / Clarté	☐	☐	☐	☐	☐
Relevance / Pertinence	☐	☐	☐	☐	☐
Information	☐	☐	☐	☐	☐

4

Thank You – Merci

special places. The power and songs they derived from vision could help them to locate lost souls.

All the Plateau tribes had shamans who were expected to cure the sick and influence the weather. Among the Kootenay, shamans often turned to blood-letting as a remedy for illness.

True to their origins, the Kootenay followed many of the spiritual customs of the plains, including the sun dance and reverence for the medicine bundle.

Most tribes engaged in story-telling and dancing during the winter. Both the Lillooet and Shuswap held masked dances, reenacting the guardian spirit's possession of a young man or woman who had embarked on a vision quest. The Interior Salish held a festival known as the ghost dance. This was celebrated whenever a band member claimed to have received a message from the land of ghosts. During the festival, a series of dances and feasts were held. Each day of this festival had certain ritual activities. The morning was devoted to fasting and ritual cleansing, noon to feasting and prayers to the Chief of the Dead and the afternoon to dancing. The evening was reserved for a smoking ceremony.

Pacific Coast Indians

Principal Tribes

There were six principal tribes of Pacific Coast Indians. The most northerly tribe was the Haida, who occupied the Queen Charlotte Islands and was the sole member of the language family called Haida.

The Tsimshian, who lived on the mainland coast directly across from the Queen Charlottes, were divided into three groups, all of whom spoke languages belonging to the Tsimshian language family. The Tsimshian lived at the mouth of the Skeena River, the Gitksan lived farther inland along the Skeena, and the Niska at the basin of the Nass River.

The southernmost Pacific Coast tribes were the Nootka and the Coast Salish. Occupying the west coast of Vancouver Island, the Nootka spoke a language belonging to the Wakashan language family. The Coast Salish were found on the eastern coast of Vancouver Island and on the mainland just opposite, from Bute Inlet to the mouth of the Columbia River. They spoke languages belonging to the Salishan language family.

Between the northern and southern tribes were found the Kwakiutl and the Bella Coola. Like the Nootka, the Kwakiutl spoke a language belonging to the Wakashan language family. They lived on the northern end of Vancouver Island and on the nearby mainland. The

Bella Coola lived on the banks of the Dean and Bella Coola rivers and on the fjords into which these rivers flowed. They belonged to the Salishan language family.

Social Organization

Compared with other tribes of Canada, the tribes of the Pacific coast had an elaborate social structure. Not only were there three distinct social strata (nobles, commoners and slaves), there was also a well-defined aristocratic class recognized as superior by reason of birth.

This social system varied from tribe to tribe. It was widespread among the Haida, Tsimshian and Kwakiutl, but less evident among the Nootka, Coast Salish and Bella Coola.

The tribes also differed in how they recognized the line of descent. Both the Haida and the Tsimshian were matrilineal, whereas the other tribes recognized descent through either the male or the female side of the family.

The basic social unit for all tribes was the extended family, whose members claimed descent from a common ancestor. Each lineage claimed specific sites for fishing, shellfish gathering, woodcutting and bark collecting. Other less tangible possessions included the right to perform certain dances, use certain names and wear particular ceremonial masks.

Most lineages had their own crests — representations of animal or supernatural beings believed to be their founders. Sometimes called totems, these crests were similar to the coats of arms of European nobility. They were displayed in as many places and in as many ways as possible. Totems could be painted on the outside of lodges or along bed platforms. They could be tatooed on the body, painted on the face, woven into ceremonial robes, or carved into ceremonial masks, wooden dishes, spoons and storage chests.

Through this dedication to the crest and supernatural ancestors, Pacific Coast tribes achieved some highly distictive and powerful art forms which today are universally admired and housed in museums throughout the world. The "multi-perspective" technique was favoured by Pacific Coast artists. Working with all sides of a storage box, for example, an artist would represent an animal simultaneously in full face, in profile, from the back, as seen from above and below, and even from the inside.

The most famous method of crest display, however, was the totem pole consisting of all the symbols that belonged to ancestral descendants. Carved from the gigantic red cedar, stylized animal and human forms sat one atop another, a visual testament to the line's history.

There were several kinds of totem poles, including the memorial pole and the house-portal pole. When a chief died, his heir erected a memorial pole as part of the process of assuming his predecessor's rights and privileges. The dramatic house-portal pole was built right into the front of the house and rose high above it, proclaiming the lineage of those who lived there. Such poles had a large opening at the base which formed the actual doorway to the house.

Poles might also symbolize some special privileges. Among the Kwakiutl and the Nootka, for example, a tall, slender pole topped by a bird-like figure signified the house of the beach owner. This position belonged only to the chief who had inherited the right to be the first to invite important visitors to a feast.

This kind of precise social grading characterized Pacific Coast society as a whole. With the exception of slaves, the members of each social group occupied a series of social positions that were graded from high to low. Among the Kwakiutl, for example, this social ranking of nobles determined the official seating arrangements at ceremonial feasts.

In all lineages, the leading position was held by the chief, usually the oldest member in the group descended in the most direct line from the lineage's ancestral founder. It was his responsibility to see that the material needs of all lineage members were satisfied.

The lowest ranking commoner in the lineage was the person most distantly related to the chief. This bottom rank nevertheless carried some privileges, including the right to participate in ceremonial feasts and use certain names belonging to the group as a whole.

Even among the Kwakiutl, Haida and Tsimshian tribes, whose societies were very formally structured, it was still possible for an individual to modify his place in the social scale. A low-ranking commoner who was also a particularly skilled canoe maker or mask carver could sometimes gain privileges beyond his rank if his work was admired by the chief. Conversely, a person who fell into disfavour would receive only minimal privileges and economic benefits. Amongst both the Coast Salish and the Bella Coola there was a considerable amount of such shifting up and down the social scale, depending on an individual's abilities.

Not only were the noblemen and the commoners graded, the lineages themselves were as well. The chief of the most powerful and prestigious lineage would therefore be chief of a village.

In each village, there were slaves owned by the various lineages. These slaves were usually taken in warfare, and, if their lineage was wealthy, they would be ransomed. Those retained by households performed menial tasks such as gathering firewood and digging for clams.

The bounty of the sea — salmon, shellfish, herring, smelt, octopus, crabs, whale and seaweed — made it possible for the Pacific coast tribes to settle in permanent locations. Unlike the Iroquoian tribes who relocated every 15 years or so, the Indians of the Pacific coast generally built permanent villages.

Some village sites show evidence of occupation over 4 000 years. They were often located on the shores of bays and inlets where they were sheltered from the ocean waves. Consisting of between 10 and 30 lodges, each village had a population of 200 to 700 people.

Fishing and Hunting Techniques

For fishing, all the coastal tribes made dip nets of nettle fibres attached to a wooden frame. These were used for salmon and for smaller fish like herring and smelt. The Salish, Tsimshian and Haida all used gill nets. These were large nets made of a special type of mesh which caught the fish under its gill covers when it tried to extract its head.

Underwater traps made of poles were often used. The general design was a funnel for channelling the fish into a box-like structure from which they could be lifted with a net.

Another salmon fishing device was the harpoon consisting of a detachable head of barbed bone connected by a short line to a wooden shaft. The Kwakiutl and the Nootka made two-pronged harpoons with compound barbed heads; the more northerly tribes used a harpoon with a single tip.

Generally using baited hooks of bone, fishermen trolled for salmon in salt water before spawning season occurred, and for cod and halibut at all times. The Haida, Tsimshian and Kwakiutl made halibut hooks of hardwood.

It was usually the women who gathered the shellfish: clams, mussels, abalones, oysters and periwinkles. Their only tool was a specially constructed stick of hardwood used for prying loose or digging up resistant shells.

While some fish was eaten fresh (broiled over open fires or beds of coals), most of the salmon caught was dried in smokehouses and packed away for later use. All the tribes used the abundant berries, which were either eaten fresh or mixed with oil and preserved.

Oil itself played a very vital part in the diet of the Pacific Coast tribes. Not only did it serve as a condiment to make the winter's dried fish more palatable, but it compensated to some extent for the low starch content in the coastal diet.

A highly valued source of oil was the *eulachon* — type of smelt about 12 centimetres long. The eulachon was so full of oil that when dried, placed upright and lit, it would burn from end to end like a candle. Also called the candlefish, it ran in the

Nass River for about six weeks beginning in the middle of March. Anxious to obtain the precious oil through trade, other tribes would visit the fishing grounds at this time and join in the excitement as spectators.

The eulachon fishery was wholly controlled by the Tsimshian and the Niska, who caught the fish with dip nets and long funnel-shaped nets with a flared opening. The production of the oil itself took about three weeks. The fish were first left a few days to ripen in wooden chests. Once the fish oil began to appear at the top of the decaying mass, hot stones would be applied to hasten the extraction process. Traditionally, the women pressed the oil by squeezing the rotting fish against their chests and letting it run into bags made from the intestines of sea mammals.

Because the Tsimshian and the Niska had a great surplus of oil, they traded it with tribes as far away as the interior of British Columbia. Today, the routes these traders travelled are still known as grease trails.

Marine Hunting

The Tsimshian, Haida and Nootka all hunted sea lion and sea otter. Equipped with harpoons, the hunters ventured forth in slim dugout canoes in search of their quarry. The most spectacular of marine hunts, however, was the Nootka's pursuit of the whale.

Even before the whaling season began in May, ritualistic preparations were made for the hunt. The burden of responsibility for rituals fell on the village chief and his wife.

The process of ritual cleansing required the couple to retreat to a traditional whaling shrine where they bathed in a cold pool. While his wife imitated the spouting and diving of the whale, the chief scrubbed at his skin with hemlock twigs until he drew blood.

Once her husband departed in the whaling canoe, the woman returned home where she lay motionless and fasted until the return of the hunters. Through this inactivity, she hoped to ensure that the whale itself would be docile.

The whaling canoe was large enough to carry a crew of eight. Directly behind the raised prow sat the harpooner. He carried a harpoon of yew wood about four metres long. Its detachable head was a sharp piece of mussel shell cemented with spruce gum between two elk antler barbs. A braided line of whale sinew attached to the harpoon head was in turn connected to long coils of rope made of twisted spruce root. Strung along this rope at regular intervals were four inflated sealskins.

When the crew sighted a whale, it approached the animal with great caution. Because the harpoon was too heavy to be hurled, the canoe had to overtake the animal. Standing in the bow, the harpooner took careful aim and plunged the harpoon deep into the whale.

Towing the carcass home could take several days — especially if the animal had headed out farther to sea during the hunt. Once successfully beached, the whale was cause for a great feast to which other chiefs were invited. The blubber was divided according to each guest's rank, and speeches were made applauding the accomplishments of the chief's family.

The Dugout Canoe

The Pacific Coast people travelled almost exclusively by water, using dugout canoes of red cedar.

The type of canoe used by the Haida, Tsimshian, Kwakiutl and Bella Coola had a high projecting bow and stern which arched over the water and prevented waves from swamping the craft. Carved figures representing the crests of the canoe owner often surmounted the bow and stern.

Canoes varied in size according to their function. A small hunting canoe for one or two men, for example, would not exceed five metres in length. Larger canoes made by the Haida were more than 16 metres long and two metres wide. Such craft were capable of carrying 40 men and two metric tons of cargo. The craftsmanship of the Haida canoe-makers was widely admired. Their canoes, therefore, were an eagerly sought after trade item when mainland and coastal tribes assembled at the Nass River eulachon fishery each spring.

The type of canoe used by the Nootka and the Salish inhabiting the coast had a bow that projected over the water. Its stern was straight and vertical. The sides of the canoe were gracefully curved in a way that prevented waves from swamping the boat.

Woodworking

The Pacific Coast Indians were excellent carpenters, despite their simple tools. They worked primarily with the soft, straight-grained cedar which split readily into planks. Coastal tribes had many uses for cedar. From it they made canoes, houses, storage boxes and ceremonial objects of all kinds, including masks and totem poles. From its inner bark they made a wide variety of clothing as well as pillows, chequered table mats, napkins and baskets.

The basic woodworking tools used by the Pacific Coast tribes were adzes and chisels (made of either stone, shell or elk horn), hardwood wedges and stone mauls. There were two types of adzes: a large version with a long handle for rough work, and a smaller one, with a D-shaped handle for finishing work.

Canoe making was considered a sacred art by all the Pacific Coast tribes. The actual construction process took three to four weeks and had its own attendant rituals, including a prescribed pattern of prayer and sexual abstinence for the canoe-maker.

The canoe's hull was stretched using a steam softening process. Water was poured into the hollow and brought to the boil with hot stones. Wooden stretchers were then inserted to hold the sides of the canoe apart while it cooled. Fine sandstone and sharkskin were used to make the outer surface as smooth as possible. While the outside of the canoe was painted black, red was the colour preferred for the interior.

Dwellings

Many houses built by Pacific Coast tribes were as massive as the cedar from which they were built. One of the largest dwellings recorded belonged to the Coast Salish. It was over 170 metres long and 20 metres wide.

Regardless of size, the fundamental house structure was the same for all tribes: a framework of logs to which outer planks were attached, running either vertically or horizontally.

The Haida, Tsimshian and northern Kwakiutl built huge, rectangular houses with gabled roofs. The outer walls of these dwellings were usually upright planks fitted into slotted sills. Heavy posts at the front and back of the house held up huge ridgepoles which in turn supported overlapping layers of roof planking. The doorway in the side of the house facing the beach was round or oval. Particularly among the Haida, the portal and corner posts were intricately carved with household crests, while outer wall paintings glorified ancestral founders.

The Nootka, Bella Coola and Salish relocated regularly from one fishing site to another. They built their homes so that the outer wall of horizontal planking formed an easily detachable shell. With each move, the roof and wall planks were stripped and then lashed to the new frame with flexible twigs.

The interior layout of the houses varied from tribe to tribe. Because the houses were spacious, they could accommodate several families, each with their own separate living area and hearth. The largest houses of the Salish consisted of individual walled-off apartments. The Haida built wooden sleeping platforms into the inner walls of their tiered dwellings. The Kwakiutl, Bella Coola and Nootka had raised shelves running along the walls. These were used for both sleeping and storage.

For the most part, people sat on mats of woven cedar bark. Wooden boxes were frequently used to store clothing, ceremonial masks, eulachon oil and whale blubber. Some boxes were so sturdily constructed that they were watertight and could be used as cooking vessels. Northern storage boxes like the Haida's tended to be squarer and squatter than those made by the Nootka and the Kwakiutl. The Haida carved their clan crests on the top, bottom and sides of the box. The high, narrow containers of the Nootka and Kwakiutl were decorated with inlays of sea otter teeth.

Dishes were usually trough-like in shape and were hollowed out from blocks of alder, a wood that did not spoil the taste of food. Spoons were made of mountain goat horn and of wood.

Clothing

Whenever weather permitted, the men went naked. Tsimshian women wore skirts of buckskin, but elsewhere women's skirts were woven of cedar bark that had been shredded to produce a soft fibre. Neither men nor women had footwear of any kind. In rainy weather the coastal people donned woven bark raincapes and wide-brimmed hats woven of spruce root. Those made by the Tsimshian had striking patterns in the weave, while the Nootka decorated their hats with paintings of whaling scenes.

The Nootka and Kwakiutl also made a distinctive long robe woven of yellow cedar bark. Some of their robes were interwoven with mountain goat wool. The most luxurious had borders of sea otter fur. Another highly prized robe was the Chilkat blanket, a trade item popular with all coastal tribes. Woven by the Alaskan Chilkat Indians, these deeply-fringed wraps were richly dyed and embroidered, making them suitable for ceremonial robes.

Spiritual Beliefs and Ceremonies

The Pacific Coast tribes strongly believed in the interconnection between the human and animal worlds. Many of the transformation masks used in their religious ceremonies illustrated this link. Ingeniously crafted, these masks opened and closed to reveal either a human or animal face as the wearer pulled the strings. The crests of the various lineages often took animal form. Both the Bella Coola and the Kwakiutl believed that their ancestors had come down from the heavens in animal cloaks and masks.

All Pacific Coast tribes believed that salmon were actually supernatural beings who lived beneath the sea in human form. When the salmon run began, the "'Salmon People", who lived beneath the waters, would become fish and sacrifice themselves for human beings. This belief gave birth to many rituals, including a welcoming ceremony honouring the first salmon of the year with an address and offerings befitting a high-ranked chief. Respect for the salmon extended to its very bones, every single one being returned to the water so that the "Salmon People" might wholly resurrect themselves.

The guardian spirits who appeared to young men in their vision quests often took animal form. Followers of special occupations were inspired by a particular spirit. Thus, canoe-makers had woodpeckers as guardian spirits; fishermen had salmon; hunters had wolves; and shamans had mythical serpents.

The Pacific Coast shamans practised various curing rituals. The long-haired Haida shamans used a special bone tube to blow away sickness and catch lost souls. In their search for souls gone astray, groups of Salish shamans mimed voyages made by spirits canoes. Nootka shamans dived to the bottom of the sea to do battle with the sea spirits who stole souls.

The coastal peoples' love of ceremony reached its peak during the winter months when spirits were thought to walk amongst the living. There was ample time for feasting, dancing and drama, as the bountiful harvest from the sea ensured five months' winter leisure.

Winter ceremonies were often organized by secret societies whose members had undergone arduous initiation rites to gain the protection of a powerful guardian spirit. In general, only people of high rank could belong to these societies and participate in the dramas which reenacted the spirit's possession of the initiate. These rituals were highly developed among the Kwakiutl who had three separate secret societies: the Shamans' Society, "The-Ones-Who-Returned-From-Heaven", and the *Nutlam*.

Fully exploiting the suggestive powers of firelight, the Kwakiutl dramas made great use of visual illusion and stage effects. Magnificently carved transformation masks enabled actors to change character in full view of the audience, while trap doors in the floor made speedy disappearances possible. Actors threw their voices by means of hollow kelp tubes concealed beneath the floor boards. Puppet monsters flew across the stage suspended on ropes; wooden crabs scuttled about on rollers.

The *potlatch* was a ceremony common to all Pacific Coast tribes. The chief of one lineage or tribe would customarily invite outside dignitaries to this celebration which combined feasting, dancing and gift-giving.

It is thought that the word potlatch may be derived from the Nootka word *pachitle*, meaning to give. Every potlatch culminated with the host chief offering presents to his guests, the worth of each gift corresponding to the guest's social ranking. The more material wealth a chief distributed, the greater was his prestige. Canoes, slaves, carved dishes and eulachon oil were all given away.

When the high-ranking guests returned the favour, holding their own potlatches, they were expected to give even more lavishly. Otherwise, they would be shamed. A chief who impoverished himself through lavish potlatch giving and feasting could therefore count on this wealth being returned, and even increased, when he attended subsequent potlatches as a guest.

But the distribution of material wealth was only one element in the potlatch ceremony. The main reason for every potlatch was to confirm in public that an individual's social status had changed. A chief might therefore give a potlatch when his daughter came of age, or when his heir assumed one of the ancestral hereditary titles. The right to dance the dances and sing the songs given by the supernatural ancestors had to be affirmed and acted out before a public gathering. The potlatch was consequently a vital and integral part of the social structure of the Pacific Coast tribes.

Indians of the Mackenzie and Yukon River Basins

Principal Tribes

Twelve principal tribes of Indians lived in the vicinity of the Mackenzie and Yukon River basins. All these tribes spoke languages belonging to the Athapaskan language family.

The Chipewyan ranged from north of the Churchill River all the way west to Great Slave Lake and controlled the largest amount of territory. To the south and west were the Beaver who lived in the basin of the Peace River.

The Slave (or Slaveys) ranged from west of Great Slave Lake as far west as the Mackenzie River. The lake-dotted land from the east end of Great Slave Lake to the eastern shore of Great Bear Lake was the territory of the Yellowknife. To their southwest were the Dogrib who occupied the land between these two great northern lakes.

West and northwest of Great Bear Lake lived the Hare. To their west were the Kutchin who occupied the basins of the Pelly and Porcupine rivers, thus taking up much of what is today the Yukon interior. The Han and the Tutchone occupied what is today the southern Yukon.

South of the Tutchone were the Kaska and the Mountain, who lived in the mountainous country to the west of the Mackenzie River. The most southern of the tribes was the Sekani, who dwelt on the eastern slopes of the Rockies in what is now northern Alberta.

Social Organization

The homeland of these northern tribes was vast, taking up over one-quarter of Canada's total land mass. Because game was so scarce, however, the people lived a semi-nomadic existence, following the scattered populations of migratory animals.

Winters were longer and more severe than those experienced by southern tribes. Forests were not dense; the trees were not sturdy. Above the eastern treeline, where the windswept tundra offered no protection against the elements, no fuel source was readily available.

Because the people were primarily occupied with day-to-day survival, their social organization took a simple form. Tribes were divided into several independent bands, each consisting of different family groups who worked together. Each band hunted a separate territory. Individual boundaries were defined by tradition and use. Family and local groups used their own particular sections of this band territory.

The position of band leader was not rigidly fixed. Rather, a leader was selected according to a band's needs at a particular time. Thus, on a caribou hunt, the most proficient hunter would be chosen leader. For raids on neighbouring tribes, the most courageous warrior assumed responsibility for strategy and attack. In times of crisis, when illness or famine prevailed, the people turned to the community shaman.

Hunting

In the Mackenzie River basin the most sought after big game animals were moose, both woodland and barren-ground caribou, and mountain sheep. Each of these species had its own ranges.

Moose, for example, abounded in the marshy woodland territory of the Slave Indians. Caribou, on the other hand, left the bushlands occupied by the Dogrib to go north to the barrenlands each summer. The Dogrib would follow the caribou herds to the edge of the barrens and then return to their own bushland to await the animals' migration.

Woodland caribou and mountain sheep were found in the territory occupied by the Kaska west of the Mackenzie River. In the territory of the Hare, however, wildlife was sparse. This tribe subsisted primarily on small game and fish.

When hunting moose, the northern tribes used techniques similar to those of the Woodland Indians. The Slave, for example, enticed the moose by imitating a moose call using a birch bark tube. Another tactic was to rub a large bone or piece of antler against a tree trunk in imitation of the male moose. When a moose emerged to confront the intruder in its territory, the hunter slew the animal with bow and arrow.

Moose were also hunted when the snow was deep and its surface covered with a crust of ice. With snowshoes strapped to his feet, the hunter could travel swiftly over frozen terrain. The moose, however, broke through the crust with every step, tiring itself as it lunged forward. Easily overtaking his quarry, the hunter often had dogs to help him keep the animal at bay while he readied his bow.

The most widespread device for catching game was a simple snare made of plaited rawhide thongs. Northern hunters like the Kutchin built elaborate routing fences with stakes and brush. These fences were used to stampede prey into an area where snares had been set to entrap the animals.

Tribes like the Chipewyan and Yellowknife followed caribou year-round as the large herds drifted from the forest lands to the barrenlands according to season. During the caribou migration, hunters would round up the animals and drive them into lakes or streams. In the water, spearmen in canoes slaughtered the floundering beasts. Below the treeline, corrals were used extensively to trap the caribou. Men, women and children were all employed in driving the animals through the entrance of a corral built with tree trunks and brush. Once trapped, the animals were killed with spears or arrows. The Kutchin took great care in building corrals of this kind. Because their land was underlain with permafrost, setting up fences was difficult work. Fences were therefore maintained for many years and bequeathed to the owner's children.

In late winter, when the snow was deep, caribou were run down by hunters wearing snowshoes. Snaring, however, was the most common method of winter hunting. Snares were sometimes tied to a short pole which the animal would drag until it became entangled in the trees. Thus caught, the animal could be easily speared.

Similar methods were used to catch the wood buffalo, which ranged the lands west of Great Slave Lake and the valleys of the southern tributaries of the Liard River. Wood buffalo were also driven into bogs where they could be killed.

The keen-eyed mountain sheep were not easy prey, for they roamed remote mountain crags and peaks. Hunters therefore had to climb above the sheep and descend upon them. Bears were killed for food often during the early winter when they were hibernating and their flesh was most tasty. Muskrat and beaver were usually snared or netted near the entrance to their homes.

In winter, freezing solved the problem of how to keep meat. It was necessary, however, to protect meat caches from the ravages of the wolverine. Most tribes cached their meat high in a tree with its trunk peeled of bark, making it too slippery for scavengers to climb.

In summer, meat was cut into thin strips and dried in the sun. Some of this dried meat was pounded into a powder; mixed with fat and stored in bags in much the same way as the pemmican of the Plains Indians.

Fishing

In the subsistence economy of the northern peoples, fishing was also important. The Slave, who lived along the Mackenzie River, caught fish in great quantities. The Kutchin had regular seasonal fishing stations along the Mackenzie. The Nahani of the mountains preferred meat, but they did fish the mountain streams when game grew scarce. The Hare, however, fished very little.

During the spring breakup many fishermen travelled to the small lakes away from the muddy Mackenzie. The Dogrib, for example, camped on the shores of Lac la Martre or along the chain of large lakes bordering the Canadian Shield. In summer, when the water level of the Mackenzie subsided, they returned to their traditional fishing spots.

Twine, made from the inner bark of the willow, was used for nets and lines. Nets were set with floats and stones in summer. In winter, nets were placed under the ice. Ice chisels were valuable tools made by attaching sharpened tips of moose antler to long poles. The poles were crafted thicker at the base to add weight to each thrust. The Yellowknife made chisel heads out of copper and traded them with both the Dogrib and the Hare.

Fishing hooks were made of wood, bone, antlers and claws. Sharpened goose bones or jawbones of large fish were also very effective when baited with minnows.

Spear fishing was another seasonal activity. In winter, holes were chiselled through the ice. Fishermen used pointed sticks of birch for spears. The Kutchin had a spear with a double gaff like that used by the Inuit. The points on the Slave's spears were made of sharpened bone with a row of barbs or beaver teeth attached.

Weapons

Many varieties of bow and arrow were used throughout the region. Around Great Bear Lake, the Hare, Yellowknife and Dogrib used bows of dried willow, about 1.5 metres long. With a shaft about as thick as the little finger, the arrow was feathered on one end and tipped with sharpened bone, stone or copper on the other. Some blunt arrows were designed to stun game like ptarmigan or grouse. One type of Kutchin bow was different and resembled that used by the Inuit. It was made of three pieces of wood joined together and reinforced with a strong lashing of twisted sinew. With practice, a hunter could shoot an arrow accurately a distance of 30 metres.

Clothing

Clothing was usually made of caribou, moose or deerskin. While moose was the hide most commonly used, the Kaska often substituted sheepskin. The Chipewyan and the Kutchin favoured caribou skin. It took about 10 skins to make a complete outfit for one man, consisting of a robe, shirt, leggings, moccasins, breech cloth, cap and mittens.

In general, men wore wide shirts that hung to the knees and were decorated with several rows of fringe. The deerskin shirts of the Chipewyan, however, were worn like a poncho, often with a long point at the front and back. Some of the Kutchin's caribou shirts were tapered like those of their neighbours, the Inuit. These shirts had an attached hood, a short waist and long tails at front and back.

For formal dress, most Athapaskans wore V-tailed shirts, leggings and moccasins, all brightly embroidered with dyed porcupine quill or moosehair. From Alaska eastward, moccasin trousers — leggings to which the moccasins were attached — were common.

Women's dress was essentially the same, with the exception of the longer shirt. Kutchin women sometimes enlarged the backs of their shirts so they could carry their babies against the warmth of their naked backs.

The women prepared caribou and moose skins in two ways: one for winter and one for summer. For winter use, shirts, leggings and robes all had hair left on for extra warmth. Caribou hair is hollow and is an excellent insulator, and the women especially prized skins taken in the fall. By then, the injuries caused by botflies had healed over and the winter coat had grown.

When making summer clothing, women would scrape the hair off hides, and later tan them with a mixture of animal brains. Sometimes a smoke tanning process was used, both sides of the hide being smoked over a slow fire.

For thread, women used tenderloin sinew from the moose or caribou. They also made the multi-purpose *babiche* (rawhide thong). Babiche was used for pulling toboggans, for lashing down loads and for snowshoe webbing. Ropes of braided babiche made snares strong enough to hold a bear.

Dwellings

Because the northern tribes led a nomadic existence, their dwellings were simple in design and easily erected. The pole structure and hide covering could be carried from place to place. The Sekani, for example, built conical lodges of poles covered with spruce bark, or simple lean-tos layered with bark, skins or brush.

In summer the Slave lived in conical lodges covered with brush or spruce bark. Two families would usually pitch their lodges beside each other, so that they had a common entrance and fireplace in the centre. The Slave's winter dwelling was a low, oblong cabin of poles. For improved insultation, its walls were chinked with moss and its roof covered with spruce boughs.

Because most Kutchin did not travel much in winter, they were able to build a more permanent dwelling. It was dome-shaped with an opening at the top for a smoke hole. For added insulation, they banked snow around the outside wall and used a second layer of skin covering. Those Kutchin who did travel in winter to hunt caribou used double-skinned, dome-shaped tents. These tents were easy to transport and erect.

Cooking was done by the hot stone method in vessels made of birch bark, closely wound willow or spruce root. Birch bark was used to make containers for drinking or carrying water. Spoons were made from horn, and plates from bark peeled at the campsite.

Modes of Transport

Canoes for summer travel were built in the spring when the sap was rising and the bark easy to peel in large pieces. While birch bark was the preferred material, the birch did not grow as large in the northern regions as it did in the eastern woodlands. Nevertheless, many Athapaskans were able to construct long, elegant canoes, using spruce gum to seal the seams between the smaller, individual pieces of bark.

In southern regions, spruce bark, stripped in one big piece from the biggest spruce available, was used to make larger canoes. The ends of the bark were pinched together and sewn with spruce root. Spruce gum was used to waterproof the seams. The canoe's centre was spread with thwarts of birch. For both spruce and birch bark canoes, peeled and shaved U-form ribs were then placed in the bottom to give strength to the craft. Tribes in the Mackenzie region sometimes used large canoes covered with moose hide.

The Slave canoe had a high bow to cut through waves in rough water. Both eastern and western tribes of Athapaskans, including the Hare, the Dogrib and the Kutchin, decked over the forward parts of their canoes to prevent them taking in water. Some tribes also decked over the sterns of their canoes.

In winter, the hunters and their families hauled their possessions on toboggans or built-up basket sleds. These were made of green birch wood which was steamed and bent at the ends before drying. The planks were lashed side by side and turned up at the front. The northern Kutchin constructed sleds with runners resembling those of the Inuit. Made of a heavy wood, the two runners were bound together with crossbars and armoured with bone or frozen mud to give them a good sliding surface.

Since snow covered the ground from September to the end of May, snowshoes were used by all tribes. Several features made the northern snowshoe distinct from those used in other parts of Canada. They were narrower and longer than the snowshoes used in the eastern woodlands and measured up to two metres in length. Some were made of one slat of birch wood bent to give a rounded front and a pointed tail. Many, however, were made of two pieces of wood spliced together at the top with babiche. The front ends were bent up slightly to prevent the snowshoes from catching on brush under the snow. The babiche lacing was most often woven in a tight hexagonal pattern. Among the eastern Athapaskans, snowshoes were highly decorated, often with paint and strings of shells. The western tribes frequently had amulets woven into the snowshoes' babiche to keep the wearer safe from unfriendly spirits.

Spiritual Beliefs and Ceremonies

All the northern tribes believed in guardian spirits that would protect them in hard times. The Sekani believed, for example, that the guardian spirit a young man obtained in his vision quest would help him only in times of dire need. If he were lucky, later in life he might obtain further guardian spirits on whom he could count at all times. Such fortunate individuals usually became shamans in the community.

Shamans often exercised great power in northern bands. All shamans were able to summon helpful animal spirits to guide them in their efforts to heal the sick. Among the Slave, shamans attempted to extract the disease-causing object by means of massage or suction. Shamans also predicted the weather and knew where game could be found. Hunters who had poor luck often requested the services of a shaman to help bring about a change of fortune.

The Kutchin used animal scapulas to determine whether or not a hunt would be successful. The ashes of a burnt arrow would be placed on a moose shoulder blade and set on fire. The shaman, very often an elderly woman, covered herself and the burning charcoal with a blanket. If she smelled burning meat, the hunt would be successful. The pattern made by the fire on the bone indicated the route to be taken by the hunters.

Like the Woodland Indians, all northern tribes followed prescribed ritual procedures in hunting and butchering game and disposing of the bones. Bears, in particular, were treated with great respect. Among the more westerly Athapaskan tribes, the lynx, wolf and wolverine were considered special ceremonial animals.

Tribes practised some group ceremonials, particularly after the killing of certain animals such as the bear and the otter. Winter solstice festivals featured feasting, singing, dancing, drumming, racing competitions and games of strength, like wrestling. The Hare regularly held two ceremonials: a lunar feast on the occasion of each new moon and a memorial feast for the dead a year after burial. All Yukon tribes had a special memorial feast for the dead, usually held on the first anniversary of the person's death.

Both the Slave and the Chipewyan believed that after death the soul made a long journey across a lake in a stone canoe. If the deceased had led a good life, the canoe travelled safely to an enchanted island, rich in game and firewood. But if the deceased had led an evil life, the canoe would sink and the soul would be doomed to spend eternity in cold water.

The Newcomers

First Encounters

The first Europeans encountered by North American Indians were Norse seamen. Although Viking settlement was never extensive, a colony was established at L'Anse aux Meadows in the northeast tip of Newfoundland about A.D. 1000. Keeping mostly to the northern regions, the Norse had ended their attempts at settlement in Greenland by the early 1400s.

Not until the voyage of Columbus in 1492 did Europeans come again to the eastern shores of North America. Attracted by the teeming cod of the Grand Banks, Basque, Breton, Spanish, Portuguese, French, Irish and English fishermen returned each summer to fish the waters off the Atlantic coast and dry-cure their catch on the adjacent shores.

So well established were these visits that when Jacques Cartier entered Chaleur Bay in 1534, he was greeted by Micmac Indians holding aloft beaver skins on sticks, inviting the French explorers ashore to trade goods. Cartier responded by firing two cannon over the Indians' heads. Undaunted, a delegation of 300 Micmac returned the next day and bartering got under way. Knives, beads and hatchets were traded for furs.

On this same voyage, Cartier encountered a fishing party of Iroquois journeying down the St. Lawrence from their village of Stadacona, where Quebec City now stands. He captured the chief's two sons and, promising to return the next year, he took the young men with him to France.

It was these two youths who piloted Cartier up the St. Lawrence to Stadacona the following year. Cartier also visited the Iroquoian settlement of Hochelaga, on the site of present-day Montreal. There he read the gospel to the Indians.

Returning to Stadacona, Cartier and his crew built a small fort, subsequently becoming the first modern Europeans to spend an entire winter in North America. The harshness of the land soon took its toll; 25 of Cartier's men died of scurvy during their stay. In March, however, the Iroquois gave Cartier a potion made from the fronds of white cedar that cured those who had survived.

Despite the fact that the Indians had helped him, Cartier later captured their chief, Donnacona, his two sons and seven other Iroquois. Although Cartier again promised to come back the following spring, it was in fact six years before he returned. Most of the Indians he had abducted had died. This tragedy left a legacy of distrust. Cartier's attempts to establish a small colony were consistently thwarted by angry Indians. Unable to brook the constant harassment, Cartier and his men returned to France in 1542.

Even though Cartier's colonists had withdrawn, expeditions of European fishermen continued to visit the east coast. In addition to fishing, they engaged in trade and bartering for furs with the Woodland Indians of the Maritimes.

The French fashion for beaver hats gave this trade a sharp incentive and by 1581 a cargo of New World beaver furs could fetch a high price in Paris. Motivated by profit, French adventurers voyaged to North America for lucrative beaver pelts.

With the fur trade intensified, the Algonkian-speaking hunters became increasingly aware of the advantages of having European manufactured goods. The Frenchmen's iron was stronger than either bone or antler; the musket was more effective than the bow and arrow. As the Indians gradually began to spend more time securing pelts for trade, they spent less time on traditional subsistence activities. Thus, European biscuits and preserved foods became partial substitutes for the meat, fish and berries that had previously made up their whole diet.

The fur trade had other repercussions on traditional lifestyles and economic activities. Armed with more effective weapons acquired from European newcomers, Indian hunters soon reduced animal populations substantially on the east coast. Because the demand for furs led hunters farther afield, bands found themselves intruding on the territory of other tribes. These intrusions gave a new and dangerous edge to intertribal warfare, particularly in view of the lethal weapons the Indians now possessed.

By the time Champlain sailed up the St. Lawrence in 1603, the Algonkin, Montagnais and Malecite he met were all eager to trade.

In 1608 Champlain decided that the St. Lawrence was the key to the richest fur country and founded the settlement called Quebec (today's Quebec City). With the construction of that settlement, contact between Europeans and Canada's native people was permanently established.

This permanent settlement of European newcomers brought about changes in the various native cultures. Virtually no aspect of Indian life remained untouched by contact with Europeans. Even the Indians' spiritual beliefs slowly began to erode.

Religious Missions

Jesuit missionaries followed Champlain to the New World where they lived among various tribes, seeking Christian converts and recording their experiences and impressions. The Jesuits compiled these records into reports which they sent periodically to their superiors in France. These reports were eventually consolidated in 73 volumes (called the *Jesuit Relations*) which have become a primary source for researchers examining the early history of Canada's native people.

Besides seeking converts, Jesuits and Sulpicians (another religious order) also undertook the first attempts at full-scale assimilation of the Indian into French culture. The plan was to remove children from their home environment and educate them in live-in schools, either in France or in one of the new settlements. This scheme was not very successful, however, as all the students eventually returned to their people.

The Ursuline nuns made similar attempts with Indian girls, but their efforts were likewise abandoned when the nuns observed the girls becoming ill and depressed in their new surroundings.

In the late 17th and mid-18th centuries the Jesuits successfully established Christian villages among Indian people. The present-day Quebec reserves of Caughnawaga, St. Regis and Lorette all had their origins in this tutelary system of the Jesuit missionaries.

The Ravages of Disease

The spiritual and material impact of the Europeans was reinforced by the devastating effects of disease. Insanitary conditions and rotten food on European ships hastened the spread of any contagious disease among the passengers. Explorers, traders, settlers and missionaries brought a host of diseases to which the Indian people had no immunity.

By the end of the 16th century many communities were destroyed by disease. Some historians have estimated that within a 200-year period, Indian populations were reduced by as much as 95 per cent. Typhoid, diphtheria, plague, influenza, measles, tuberculosis, venereal disease and scarlet fever killed thousands. Smallpox was particularly virulent among the Montagnais, and by 1640 it had reduced the Huron population in southern Ontario by half.

In face of the horrors of these new diseases, Indian shamans were virtually powerless. Traditional cures such as the sweat-house often served simply to spread the disease. The more zealous French missionaries were quick to exploit the shamans' failures, ridiculing their impotence and thus undermining still further the traditional spiritual base of Indian life.

Intertribal Conflict

The fur trade aggravated the long-standing enmity between the Huron and the Iroquois. The desire for blood revenge was replaced by the desire to dominate territory for lucrative trapping and a concerted effort to monopolize trade with Europeans. Through their established trade connections with the Algonkin along the Ottawa River, the Huron managed to establish a monopoly on furs sold to the French. This gave them great power and influence.

By the 1630s the five tribes of the Iroquois confederacy found themselves in not nearly so fortunate a situation, having exhausted most of the supply of fur-bearing animals in their own territory. Thus they began to look enviously on the more productive lands of the Huron.

Devastated by the smallpox epidemics of 1637-1641, the Huron lost many of their experienced leaders, leaving them more vulnerable to Iroquois attack. In 1644, the Iroquois captured three canoe flotillas transporting furs to the French. A subsequent attack in March of 1649 effectively shattered the Huron nation. Many Huron fled west and were absorbed by other tribes. But essentially, the power of the Huron was ended for all time.

The Iroquois did not stop with the destruction of the Huron nation. Six months later they moved against the Tobacco nation and in 1650 dispersed the Neutral and cleared the Ottawa River of the Algonkin.

The Iroquois did not confine their hostilities to Indian tribes. Their hatred of the French dated back to 1609 when Champlain, assisting the Algonkin and their Huron allies, had routed a band of 200 warriors. The enmity engendered by that single incident was to have historical consequences lasting nearly 100 years. Not the least of these was the Iroquois tribe's continual harassment of the French settlements at Montreal, Trois-Rivières and Quebec City.

French versus English

For more than 150 years the French and English competed for control of land and trade in Canada. French "coureurs de bois", many of them part Indian, penetrated northern Ontario to the Great Lakes and beyond, seeking new sources of furs.

In 1670 the King of England granted the Hudson's Bay Company control of all lands draining into the great bay for which the company was named. From that point, competition between the two nations for Indian furs became vigorous.

Traders representing the two powers advanced through the continent, everywhere repeating the tragic scenario that had been enacted in eastern Canada and along the St. Lawrence. Indians who engaged in trade became increasingly dependent on manufactured goods, while firearms and disease took their toll on human and animal life. Intertribal rivalries flared. The Cree and Assiniboine, for example, gradually moved west and north in search of more furs, displacing other tribes in the process.

When Montreal fell to the British in 1760, ending French rule in Canada, the articles of capitulation stated that the former Indian allies of the French should be neither penalized nor disturbed in their possession of lands.

Three years later, in the Royal Proclamation setting out the boundaries of the newly-acquired province of Quebec and those of the American colonies, Indian rights were more clearly defined. The proclamation specifically declared a huge area of the country between the

Mississippi and the Appalachians to be "Indian territory". Purchases or settlements of that land were strictly forbidden without special "leave and licence" obtained from the Crown.

During the American Revolution and later again in the War of 1812, the British sought Indian aid against American troops. Indian forces under commanders like Joseph Brant (*Thayendanega*) and *Tecumseh* played a significant role in the military defence of Canada.

Indian Rights

After the American Revolution, the Royal Proclamation of 1763 ceased to have any bearing on relations between Indians and Americans. In Canada, however, the proclamation had established a framework for undertaking any future settlements of Indian lands. Thereafter, it was accepted policy that while title to the land mass of Canada was vested in the Crown, the indigenous peoples maintained an underlying title to use and occupy the land. No settlement of land could be undertaken, therefore, until the Indian rights had been surrendered in negotiation between the Crown and Indian occupants.

Between 1763 and 1800, 24 treaties were signed with different groups of Indians, most of them covering the fertile agricultural lands along the north shore of Lake Ontario. The Indians involved did not initiate these treaties, nor did they greatly influence the terms. The objective was simply to clear the land of the Indian title acknowledged in the Royal Proclamation.

At first, lump sum cash payments were made for these land surrenders. Later, however, the Crown undertook to set aside reserves and provide annuities and other benefits for the Indian people surrendering title to their land.

The general European belief was that Indian hunters and gatherers failed to realize the full potential of the land. Some settlers assumed that because the Indians did not cultivate the land, they placed no value on it.

The Western Fur Trade

In eastern Canada intensive hunting and trapping had dire consequences. Pushed aside by settlement, the Indian people found themselves in northern reaches where large game was scarce, if indeed it existed at all. By 1820 the moose population had disappeared from northern Ontario, not to reappear until 1890. One group of Ojibway moved out into the prairies to survive. Those who remained in Ontario had to subsist on small game such as marten, muskrat and hare.

In the west where game was still abundant, the Hudson's Bay Company and the North-West Company competed fiercely for the Indians' favour. The two companies established a line of trading posts right across the prairies, reaching as far north as Great Slave Lake by 1786. Each post was equipped with a complement of manufactured goods, firearms and alcohol — all of which fostered Indian dependence on the trader.

As trade moved west, so too did virulent diseases. In 1781 smallpox reduced the Indian population on the prairies by one-third.

With the westward advance of the frontier came wanton slaughter of the buffalo. Often the carcasses were left to rot and the hides taken to be fashioned into robes. By the late 1880s the vast buffalo herds of the plains had greatly diminished.

On the Pacific coast, the Indian people were visited by American, Spanish and British traders from the 1770s onwards. The early trade in sea otter skins was initially highly profitable to Europeans, who discovered a ready market for pelts in China. Soon, however, the coastal Indians learned to concentrate the trade by gathering supplies from a wide area. Having established this monopoly, they were able to increase their prices, substantially reducing the traders' profit margin.

While at first the Indians sought to trade for metal, they eventually began to barter for European clothing, especially blankets, and for the widespread rum and firearms. The introduction of firearms aggravated intertribal warfare, while smallpox and venereal disease severely weakened whole populations.

Ironically, the early phases of European trade gave the Pacific Coast cultures a positive stimulus. With their penchant for accumulating and displaying wealth, the coastal tribes put their newly acquired riches toward increasingly elaborate ceremonials like the gift-giving potlatch. To show off their wealth to advantage, chiefs required new ceremonial objects such as robes, masks and carved chests. As a result, artistic production flourished, particularly wood carving, where the now widespread European tools proved popular among Indian artisans.

With the influx of settlers, the Indians were pushed out of land which had been slated for cultivation. Agricultural settlement destroyed many traditional food gathering grounds. The camas grounds of the Fort Victoria area, for example, were torn up by the plow.

Missionaries brought schemes for conversion and acculturation. William Duncan, an Anglican missionary, built an entire community — *Metlakatla* — devoted to turning small groups of Indians into industrious citizens akin to the Europeans.

Experiments in Acculturation

The year 1830 is generally considered to be the beginning of the modern system of Indian administration in Canada. From that date, Indian settlement on reserves began under government guardianship.

After the War of 1812 the British no longer feared invading forces. Indians therefore ceased to be useful as military allies. Responsibility for Indian administration was accordingly removed from the military and put in the hands of civilians. The ultimate goal of this new civilian administration was the complete assimilation of scattered Indian bands into communities.

Various methods of achieving assimilation were considered. Some believed that Indians should be placed among the settlers to learn through imitation. Others felt that they should be isolated on reserves where teachers, government agents and missionaries would serve as instructors.

One early assimilation experiment was tried at Coldwater, near Lake Simcoe. A group of Ojibway were gathered on the Coldwater reserve to be instructed in the agricultural arts, but the experiment failed dismally. Among the contributing factors were a general lack of understanding of Indian culture and values and the missionaries' partisan competition for adherents. Moreover, the Ojibway fishermen and hunters regarded agricultural work as demeaning. They could not appreciate the value of jobs like road building as being appropriate in the context of their culture.

In 1836 a different experiment was tried. Sir Francis Bond Head, lieutenant-governor of Upper Canada, believed that any attempts at assimilation would be hopeless.

He therefore arranged for a group of Indians to be isolated from European settlements. The site chosen was Manitoulin Island on Lake Huron. Very few Indians, however, opted to relocate there. Within a few years the government had persuaded the Indians on the island to surrender their rights to half of it so that Europeans could be settled as farmers.

During the 1840s various royal commissions looked into the plight of the Canadian Indian. Many Indians continued to lose land held on their behalf to squatters, loggers and poachers. To help combat this kind of intrusion, the Royal Commission of 1844 recommended various improvements in the administration of Indian lands.

In 1850 it was decided that stronger measures were required to protect Indians and their lands. Acts were passed to achieve this in both Lower Canada (Quebec) and Upper Canada (Ontario). In Lower Canada all Indian lands and property were vested in a commissioner of crown lands and 93 000 hectares were set aside, which eventually permitted the creation of nine new reserves. An act for Upper Canada made it an offence for anyone to deal with Indians concerning their lands, or "to enter on, take possession of, or settle on any such lands, by pretext of any right or interest in the same."

The Robinson Treaties

In the 1850s attention turned for the first time to northern areas still occupied by bands of Indian hunters. The attraction was minerals discovered along the shores of Lake Superior and Lake Huron. A commissioner, W.B. Robinson, was sent to negotiate with the Ojibway for surrender of their title to the land in question.

The treaties he negotiated were called the Robinson-Huron and Robinson-Superior treaties. Through them, the Indians agreed "to surrender, cede, grant and convey unto Her Majesty, her heirs and successors forever, all their rights, title and interest to the land, and the right to fish and hunt in the lands they surrendered, until these lands are sold or leased to individuals or companies."

An Act for "Gradual Civilization"

In 1857 an act was passed aimed specifically at assimilating Indian people into the mainstream of colonial life. The essence of this act was the concept of "enfranchisement". By forsaking his Indian heritage, an Indian man with the appropriate qualifications could enter into full citizenship. Any Indian male over the age of 21, literate in English or French, educated to an elementary level, of good moral character and free of debt could be declared to be enfranchised or "no longer deemed to be an Indian" and therefore free of distinction between himself and other citizens. To encourage such a move, enfranchised Indians would be granted "fee simple title" to as much as 20 hectares of reserve land, plus an amount of money equal to the annuities received on his behalf by the band.

During the next decade a whole range of acts relating to Indians was passed. These encouraged the Indian people to move towards the social and political level of their non-native neighbours. The acts also protected Indian lands from alienation, guarded Indians against the effects of alcohol, and provided for the management of Indian schools and monies earned from Indian lands. All this legislation was to be inherited by the new nation of Canada when it gained its independence from Britain in 1867.

The Metis Resistance

As the young Canadian government moved to establish its authority over the lands west of Ontario, it met with opposition from the Metis. Although not classified as Indians under the Indian Act, these descendants of fur traders and Indian women played a major role in the struggle for recognition of native rights as well as in the development of Canada's west. The Metis were most prominent in the prairies, where they had developed a lifestyle that combined the hunting traditions of nomadic Indians with the more settled ways of European newcomers.

Traders were dependent on the Metis buffalo hunters for their supplies. Metis buffalo hunts were highly organized affairs, involving as many as 1 500 men, women and children. The pemmican prepared by the women became the staple food of the fur trader.

As more settlers moved west, the Metis began to fear that the establishment of an agricultural society would destroy their culture. Under the leadership of Louis Riel, the Metis expelled a team of government surveyors plotting routes for incoming settlers in 1869. The Metis informed the prospective governor of the territory that he could not enter without their written permission.

Metis resistance then increased. The new governor was held at the border and the Hudson's Bay Company post at Fort Garry was seized. Now in a firm bargaining position, the Metis asked Canada for a government similar to that of the other Canadian provinces. They wanted all their property and privileges protected as well as amnesty for those who had resisted Canadian authority.

Accordingly, Canada passed the Manitoba Act in 1870. This established the province of Manitoba as part of the Canadian confederation. The act also provided that 60 000 hectares of the new province be appropriated for the families of Metis residents.

Unfortunately, the provisional Metis government had earlier executed one of its prisoners, an act that gave rise to protest in Ontario. In view of the this violation of Canadian law, the federal government was compelled to send troops to Manitoba with instructions to put an end to any insurrection. The promise of amnesty was not kept and Louis Riel had to go into hiding. Although twice elected to Canada's Parliament, he was never allowed to take his seat.

The Major Treaties

In 1871 the far western colony of British Columbia agreed to join Canada on condition that a rail link be built to the rest of the country within 10 years. At that time, the Indian people numbered perhaps 25 000 across the prairies. But non-natives now began to enter their territory in vast numbers. In 1871, to prepare the way, Canada began to obtain surrender of title to all lands that the new settlers would require.

Geographical unity was thus the driving force behind a series of "numbered" treaties concluded in rapid succession throughout the fertile belt — the area of prime agricultural land north of the American border between Lake Superior and the Rocky Mountains.

For the most part, Treaty Nos. 1 to 11 featured similar provisions. With a few subtle differences, all the western treaties provided for reserve lands, monetary payments, suits of clothing every three years to chiefs and headmen, yearly ammunition and twine payments (Treaty Nos. 1, 2 and 9 excepted) and some allowances for schooling. Treaty No. 6 was the only agreement providing for medical treatment and for "assistance in the case of pestilence or famine."

Treaty activity began in Manitoba and the Northwest Angle of the Lake of the Woods. It continued on throughout the prairies and the northwest, then back again to include all northern Ontario.

In 1871 Treaty Nos. 1 and 2 took in all the fledgling province of Manitoba, including land north and west of its initial boundaries. Under Treaty No. 1, the Chippewa and the Swampy Cree surrendered a tract of land covering some 41 750 square kilometres. Under Treaty No. 2 the negotiators secured a surrender of agricultural and timber lands to the north and west of Manitoba from the Chippewa Indians. The area ceded was 89 250 square kilometres.

The objective of Treaty No. 3, negotiated in 1873, was to secure safe passage for immigrants travelling between Ontario and Manitoba. Often referred to as the Lake of the Woods link, the territory ceded by the Saulteaux and others under Treaty No. 3 provided clear access to the west. This made future expansion and development possible.

By Treaty No. 4, known as the Qu'Appelle Treaty, the negotiators obtained a surrender of 194 000 square kilometres from the Cree and Saulteaux in 1874. This huge tract of land, later to become the province of Saskatchewan, lay between the South Saskatchewan River and the United States border.

Treaty No. 5, the Lake Winnipeg Treaty, was negotiated in 1875. The Saulteaux and the Swampy Cree surrendered 260 000 square kilometres of land surrounding lakes Winnipeg and Manitoba. The land was required because of the importance of the Saskatchewan River as a transportation route into the interior. The significance of this river route diminished, however, when the railway was built a few years later.

By Treaty No. 6 in 1876, the Plains and Wood Cree and the Assiniboine surrendered title to the rest of the mid-prairie area of Alberta (approximately 310 000 square kilometres). Only Chief Big Bear of the Plains Cree refused to sign.

In 1877 Treaty No. 7 was signed with the Blackfoot, Blood, Piegan, Sarcee and Stoney (also known as Assiniboine) tribes of the remainder of the fertile belt (southern Alberta). By that time the ban on liquor by the North-West Mounted Police had enabled the Blackfoot to recover some of their former stability and economic independence. Their chief, Crowfoot, therefore refused the government rations that the treaty commissioners normally supplied when Indian leaders were assembled for negotiations.

The Northwest Rebellion of 1885

Despite the government's attempts to clear the way for settlers, the Metis once again proved to be a stumbling block.

Although the Metis had been guaranteed land settlements in the Manitoba Act in 1870, there had been long delays in implementing this promise. Moreover, the process for carrying out these grants was beset by administrative confusion.

By 1884 many Metis were still without land security. As new homesteaders moved in, conflicts over the rights to lots made an already explosive situation worse. Coincidentally, many Indians on the prairies were also suffering from epidemics and malnutrition.

The Metis summoned Louis Riel from his work as a mission schoolteacher in Montana, asking that he lead them in their struggle for justice. Riel formulated a Bill of Rights in December 1884 and sent it to Ottawa, hoping to make government officials aware of the Metis plight. As months passed and there was no reply, many Metis grew impatient with Riel's moderate approach and agitated for military action.

Only a small fraction of the Metis population joined the rebellion, however. In response to the Metis call for support, the Cree chiefs Big Bear and Poundmaker rallied their people and joined Riel's forces. Unfortunately, Big Bear could not prevent his warriors from killing nine settlers at Frog Lake. His band then moved against Fort Pitt, surrounding it and demanding food and clothing.

The Canadian government responded by sending in 8 000 troops, and within two months the rebellion was crushed. Riel was convicted of treason in 1885 and sentenced to death. The Indians chiefs Big Bear and Poundmaker were imprisoned for two years and eight other Indians were hanged.

Treaties for the Northern Reaches

Treaty activity resumed in 1899 with Treaty No. 8. Negotiated in response to the discovery of gold in the Klondike, its objective was to provide safe passage for the thousands of newcomers seeking their fortune. More than 812 000 square kilometres were surrendered, covering the northern half of Alberta, the southern portion of the Mackenzie district in the Northwest Territories, the northwest corner of Saskatchewan and the northeast corner of British Columbia. Because of their unique geographical position and close relationship with neighbouring Alberta Indians, the Indian bands of northeastern British Columbia were also brought under this treaty.

Other than land surrenders undertaken when British Columbia was still a colony, this inclusion of the northeast corner of the province in Treaty No. 8 represents the only formal treaty activity in which the Indian people of B.C. have participated.

Treaty Nos. 9 and 10 were signed in 1905 and 1906 respectively, covering all of the remaining northern lands of the provinces. Under Treaty No. 9, the Ojibway and the Cree surrendered over 550 000 square kilometres. By Treaty No. 10, the Chipewyan and Cree surrendered to the Crown a large tract of land in northern Saskatchewan and a small area at the 55th parallel in Alberta.

The discovery of oil in the far north prompted the government to sign Treaty No. 11 with the Indians of the Northwest Territories in 1921. Slave, Dogrib, Hare and Loucheux surrendered approximately 930 000 square kilometres.

Many historians speculate that while the commissioners saw the treaties in one way, the Indians had a different perspective. Often the two groups came together with vastly different expectations. The Indians sought protection from invading land-hungry settlers and the disruptions they sensed would follow these newcomers. They sought wide ranges which they could call their own and where they could live as they had in the past. The commissioners, on the other hand, saw Indian reserves as places where Indians could learn to be settlers and farmers. For this and other reasons, the treaties left hanging many questions that are yet to be resolved.

The First Indian Act

In 1876 the Canadian Parliament passed its first consolidated Indian Act. Although there have been several major revisions, many of its provisions remain to this day.

Consolidating all previous legislation with a host of new regulations, the Indian Act gave great powers to government to control Indians living on reserves.

It was during this period that the distinction between "status" and "non-status" Indians was first formulated. (Status Indians are those who are registered with the federal government as Indians according to the terms of the Indian Act. Non-status Indians are those who are not registered.) An Indian woman who married a non-Indian, for example, was no longer considered to be an Indian within the meaning of the act. Nor were her children. The reverse situation did not hold true, however, and it became possible for non-Indian women marrying Indian men to gain actual Indian status. This blatant discrimination against Indian women lasted for nearly 100 years, until long overdue amendments to the Indian Act were passed in 1985.

Government control extended to Indian reserve lands. The act of 1876 explicitly forbade the selling, alienation or leasing of any Indian reserve land unless it was first surrendered or leased to the Crown. By an 1889 amendment, the government assumed greater control over land. This amendment was drafted specifically to permit the federal government to override any band's reluctance to have its land leased.

The Indian Act of 1876 also made provision for the election of Indian band chiefs, giving them limited authority over matters such as the allocation of land within reserves and the maintenance of roads. Essentially, these band chiefs functioned as agents of the federal government, exercising limited power within federal supervision. Nor did this uniform system take into account the great diversity of Indian people and cultures, particularly those accustomed to hereditary chieftainship.

The concept of enfranchisement was a key provision of the act, the government's ultimate aim still being the total assimilation of Canada's Indian population. Very few Indians opted to become enfranchised, however, and an 1880 amendment declared that any Indian obtaining a university degree would be automatically enfranchised. A 1933 amendment took enforced enfrachisment even further. By that amendment the government was empowered to order the enfranchisement of Indians meeting the qualifications set out in the act, even without the request of the individuals concerned.

There were still other outstanding examples of how government sought to keep the Indian in a state of wardship, regulating all aspects of existence on and off the reserve. One was the amendment of 1884 banning the celebration of the potlatch on the grounds that it was a corrupt and destructive ceremony. Not dropped from the books until 1951, this amendment resulted in many Indians going to jail. The government ban did not take into account that the potlatch was the social and cultural heart of the Pacific Coast Indians.

In 1927 yet another new restriction was put into place. In response to the Nishga Indians' pursuit of a land claim, the government passed an amendment forbidding anyone from raising money among Indians for the purpose of pursuing any claim "without the consent of the Superintendent General [of Indian Affairs] expressed in writing".

Thus, through many ways and means, the Indian Act deprived the Indian people of power and kept them locked in a state of dependency.

E.S. Curtis/Public Archives Canada

A Sarcee kitchen. In traditional Plains Indian culture, the women made pemmican, a mixture of dried, powdered buffalo meat, melted buffalo fat and berries. Packed away in tightly sewn skin bags, pemmican remained edible for years.

E.S. Curtis/Public Archives Canada

Transporting the ceremonial bag and tipi cover of a Blackfoot military society. Military societies had various important functions, including regulating life in camp and on the march.

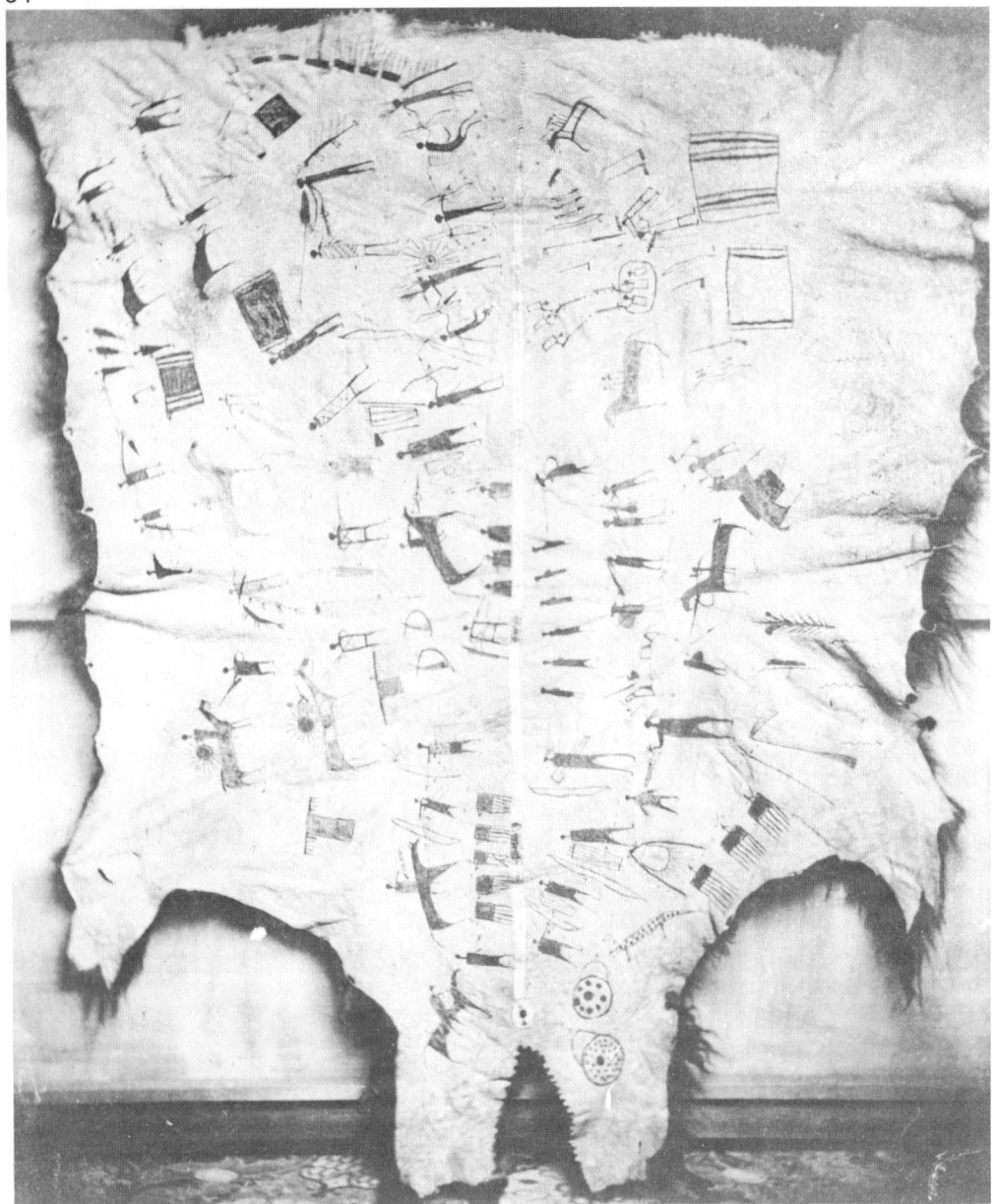

E.S. Curtis/Public Archives Canada

Blackfoot warrior's robe. Elderly Plains Indians would often paint a series of pictographs on buffalo skin to record their war deeds for all time.

E.S. Curtis/Public Archives Canada

A Piegan elder. The wisdom and experience of Indian elders were greatly valued in Plains Indian society.

E.S. Curtis/Public Archives Canada

The Cree chief Poundmaker (circa 1886).

E.S. Curtis/Public Archives Canada

Chief Crowfoot of the Blackfoot tribe was instrumental in negotiating Treaty No. 7 with the Canadian government. This photograph was taken for Crowfoot's life-time pass granted to him by the Canadian Pacific Railway.

Piegan tipi interior. This archival photograph shows the spacious interior of a ceremonial tipi. Ceremonial regalia, including medicine bundles, hang from the tipi poles.

Fishing camp at Restigouche, New Brunswick (circa 1920).

Hunter calling a moose. Woodland hunters traditionally made moose calls by rolling birch bark into a cone.

Women mending birch bark canoe at North West Angle of Lake of the Woods, Ontario (circa 1872).

E.S. Curtis/Public Archives Canada

Indian women of the Pacific coast shredded cedar bark to produce a soft fibre. They wove this fibre into material for skirts, robes and raincapes.

E.S. Curtis/Public Archives Canada

The Nootka Indians of the Pacific coast used the two-pronged harpoon for hunting seal.

The high projecting bow and stern of the Pacific Coast Kwakiutl canoe were often elaborately painted and carved with figures representing legendary ancestors.

Masked dancers participating in a Kwakiutl winter ceremonial.

E.S. Curtis/Public Archives Canada

The graceful lines of the Nootka canoe made it an excellent sea-going vessel.

E.S. Curtis/Public Archives Canada

Kwakiutl totem poles at Alert Bay (circa 1910).

Canadian Government Photo Centre

Reconstructed Iroquois longhouse in Brantford, Ontario. A False Face Society mask grimaces in the foreground.

E.S. Curtis/Public Archives Canada

A turn-of-the-century artist paints traditional Haida patterns on a hat of woven spruce root.

Canadian Government Photo Centre

Modern-day British Columbia artist Victor Mowatt works traditional Haida patterns into a cedar box.

Canadian Government Photo Centre

Indians fishing for crabs off the British Columbia coast.

Canadian Government Photo Centre

Band members at work on the Mistassini Reserve Band Council Office.

DIAND Photo

Over 75 per cent of Canada's Indian bands now administer all or parts of their education program.

DIAND Photo

Preserving native languages is an essential part of Indian education today.

DIAND Photo

DIAND Photo

Special programs have been designed to build a modern education system around the values of traditional Indian culture.

Canadian Government Photo Centre

Self-government is an essential part of the new relationship between the Indian First Nations and the federal government.

The Age of Resurgence

By the end of World War II, Canadian Indians had suffered through many decades of governmental and social neglect. Some historians have described these decades as the period during which Indians became irrelevant to Canadian society.

Hemmed in by the restrictive Indian Act, they were prevented from taking charge of their own affairs. Indeed, until the mid-1950s federal government Indian agents had control over virtually all aspects of Indian life on reserves, even to the point of issuing passes to allow Indians to leave the reserve temporarily.

Through the residential school system, the government policy of assimilation continued unabated. Removed from their homes, Indian children were not permitted to speak their own language or to practise their religious beliefs or rituals.

The late 1940s, however, marked the beginning of a new era for Canadian Indian people. Indian leaders emerged, forcefully expressing their people's desire to gain their rightful position of equality with other Canadians, and, at the same time, maintain their cultural heritage. In British Columbia, Alberta, Saskatchewan and Ontario, Indian people formed provincially-based organizations to protect and advance their interests.

Many Indian leaders drew attention to the fact that thousands of Indians had fought for their country in both world wars. Although considered good enough to fight, Indian veterans were nevertheless treated as government wards on their return home. This obvious injustice helped increase the public's awareness of Indian people's disadvantaged situation.

The Joint Committee Hearings (1946-48)

As a result of Indian efforts and public concern, in 1946 Parliament established a special joint committee of the Senate and the House of Commons to consider revisions to the Indian Act. During the following three summers the committee received briefs and representations from Indians, missionaries, schoolteachers and federal government administrators.

From these hearings the Canadian public learned just how far Indians had fallen behind all other groups of citizens in terms of living standards, health and education. Malnutrition and diseases caused by poor living conditions were widespread. Evidence also revealed that over 8 000 Indian children had no access whatever to any kind of schooling.

Many Indians addressing the committee rejected the idea of cultural assimilation into non-native society. In particular, they spoke out against the enforced enfranchisement provisions of the Indian Act.

Indians also strongly criticized the extent of powers exercised by the government over their affairs. Many groups asked that these "wide and discretionary" powers be vested in the chiefs and councillors on reserves so that they in turn could determine questions of band membership and manage their own funds and reserve lands.

In addition, Indian groups asked that the government adhere more strictly to provisions set out in the various treaties.

The 1951 Indian Act

Despite the extensive hearings, when the Indian Act was revised in 1951, it did not greatly differ from any previous legislation. The involuntary enfranchisement clause was retained, as were the provisions that determined Indian status. The Indian Act of 1951 therefore left unchanged those provisions that discriminated against Indian women on the basis of their sex. Indian women who married non-Indian men continued to lose their Indian status automatically.

The act, however, did introduce some changes. Laws banning the potlatch and other ceremonies were rescinded and Indians were given the freedom to enter public bars to consume alcohol. On the whole, however, government powers over Indian life remained formidable. Moreover, Parliament did not act on the joint committee's recommendation that a claims commission be established to hear problems arising from the fulfilment of the treaties.

Although the Indian Act continued to block the Indian people's desire for self-determination, by 1960 some definite improvements had been made in their social and economic conditions. With the provision of better health services in the mid-1950s, the status Indian population increased rapidly. In addition, many more Indian children had access to schooling, including secondary and post-secondary education.

In general, however, the living conditions of Indian people still fell far short of the standards other Canadians had come to expect as the norm.

The 1969 White Paper

In a further effort to help Indian people achieve equality with other Canadians, the federal government consulted with them extensively during 1968-69 on proposed changes to the Indian Act. The White Paper on Indian Policy which the government then proposed, was however, overwhelmingly rejected by Indian people.

Essentially, the policy called for a repeal of the Indian Act, thus ending the federal responsibility for Indians and terminating their special status. The policy also recommended that an equitable way be found for bringing the treaties to an end. In this way, the government hoped to abolish what it deemed the false separation between Indian people and the rest of Canadian society.

What the government had not fully understood was the value Indian people placed on their special status within confederation and on their treaty rights. The Indian Act thus revealed itself to be a paradox for Indian people. While it could be viewed as a mechanism for social control and assimilation, it was also the vehicle that confirmed the special status of Indians in Canada.

So vehement was the negative reaction of Indian people and the general public that the government withdrew the White Paper. Ironically, the new policy had served to fan sparks of Indian nationalism. Indian leaders from across the country united in a reaffirmation of their separateness. The Indian Association of Alberta, for example, entitled their paper of counter-proposals "Citizens Plus". In other words, Indian people wanted all the benefits of Canadian citizenship in addition to their special rights deriving from their unique trust relationship with the Crown.

The White Paper had the positive effect of clearing the air. The government sought new measures to help Indian people gain from the benefits enjoyed by Canadian society as a whole, while preserving and encouraging their unique cultural heritage.

In 1969 all Indian agents were withdrawn from Indian reserves across the country, thus ending the government's paternalistic presence on Indian lands. At this time, the government also began to fund Indian political organizations. Increasingly, these organizations focused on the need for full recognition of their aboriginal rights and renegotiation of the treaties. They believed that only in this way could they rise above their disadvantaged position in Canadian society. Accordingly, in 1970 the government began funding Indian groups and associations specifically for research into treaties and Indian rights.

Indian Control of Indian Education

In 1972 the National Indian Brotherhood (now the Assembly of First Nations) presented the government with its paper entitled "Indian Control of Indian Education". That paper advocated that Indian communities take responsibility for their children's education through their own school boards. Indian control over education was seen as essential to strengthening Indian culture and preserving Indian heritage.

The policy was adopted by the Department of Indian Affairs and Northern Development in 1973. Soon after, churches were phased out of Indian education and residential schools were closed. Special programs have since been established which attempt to build a modern educational system around the values of traditional Indian culture.

Over 75 per cent of Canada's 580 Indian bands now administer all or parts of their education programs. In schools that are still federally administered, the percentage of Indian administrators and teachers has greatly increased. In addition, both the Nishga of British Columbia and the Cree of northern Quebec have created their own school boards under provincial law.

The Cree School Board has the power to decide on the language of instruction, the curriculum and textbooks, and to hire teachers and control administration.

The James Bay and Northern Quebec Agreement

The unique power of the Cree School Board is a direct result of the 1975 James Bay and Northern Quebec Agreement — the first contemporary native land claims agreement to be reached in Canada. This

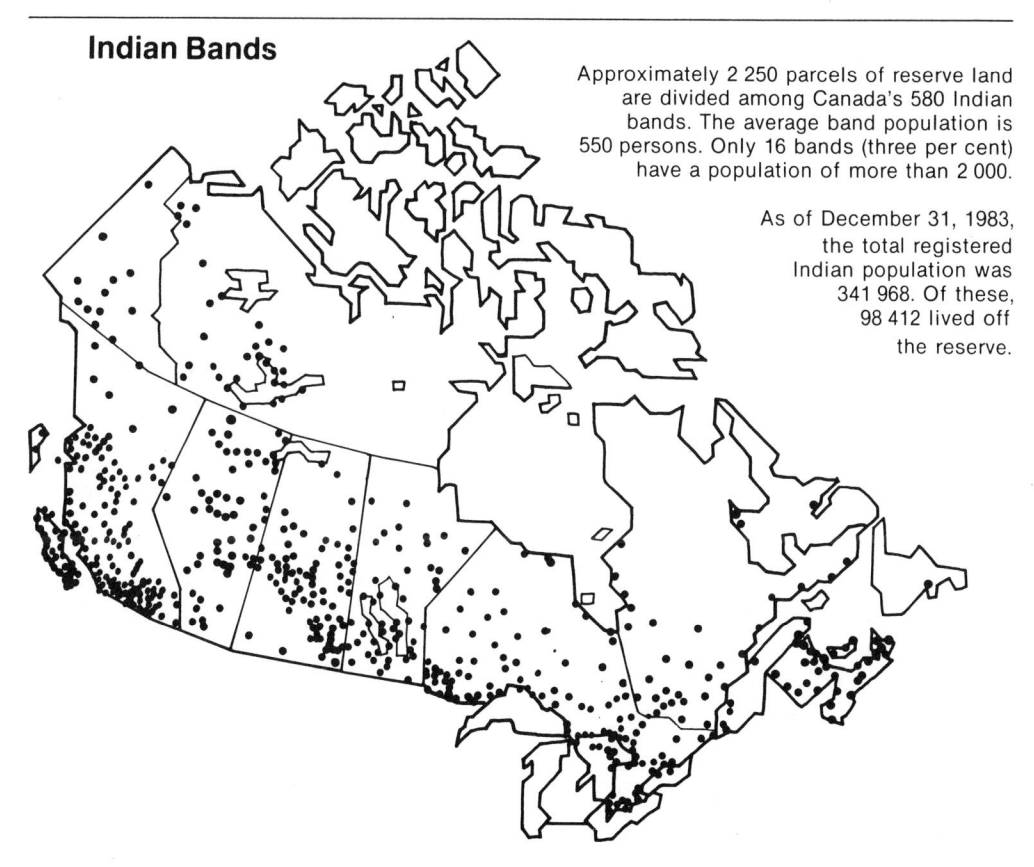

Indian Bands

Approximately 2 250 parcels of reserve land are divided among Canada's 580 Indian bands. The average band population is 550 persons. Only 16 bands (three per cent) have a population of more than 2 000.

As of December 31, 1983, the total registered Indian population was 341 968. Of these, 98 412 lived off the reserve.

agreement, and the court cases that preceded it, marked a giant step forward in terms of native peoples' assertion of aboriginal rights.

It was the Quebec government's construction of a huge hydroelectric project in the James Bay region which brought the issue of aboriginal rights to the fore. The scheme involved the blocking and diversion of several rivers, and the consequent flooding of the wilderness where the northern Quebec Cree had from time immemorial engaged in hunting and trapping.

No treaty had ever been signed, nor any surrenders of land negotiated in this part of the country. While the Cree believed they maintained some rights to the land, these were not recognized by the Quebec government. In 1972, therefore, the Cree went to court with the help of federal funding. They claimed violation of their traditional rights and asked for an injunction to stop all work on the project until their title to the land could be dealt with by negotiation.

In court the Cree argued that the completed project would severely damage the wetlands around the rivers and lakes — the primary habitat of the animals they hunted for survival. For six months Cree and Inuit hunters testified about their way of life in their own languages, while their attorneys called expert witnesses to describe the environmental devastation likely to result from the project.

In November 1973, in a judgment unparalleled in Canadian legal history, the Quebec Superior Court ruled in favour of the native peoples. The judge determined that Quebec had an unfulfilled obligation under the 1912 Quebec Boundaries Extension Act, to alienate Indian title before undertaking settlement. He also found the native petitioners' fears about injuries to their rights to be justified.

Although this decision was later reversed by the Quebec Court of Appeals, negotiations between the native peoples, the federal government and Quebec government began soon afterwards.

Under the final agreement signed in November 1975, the Cree and Inuit surrendered aboriginal title to approximately 981 610 square kilometres of the James Bay/Ungava territory. In return they were awarded $225 million over 20 years. They were also given tracts of community lands with exclusive hunting and trapping rights over large areas. In addition, provisions were made for the Cree and the Inuit to establish new systems of local government on lands set aside for their use.

The Cree School Board grew out of the agreement's provisions for native-controlled education and health authorities. The agreement also set out measures relating to policing and the administration of justice, continuing federal and provincial benefits and special social and economic development measures.

Cree funds from the agreement are administered by the Cree Regional Authority. Through the authority, the Cree benefit from such profit-oriented businesses as Air Creebec and the Cree Construction Company.

As this settlement shows, native claims are not simply concerned with the loss of a traditional way of life. Native people see claims settlements as the means to make some of the economic and social changes they desire. Settlements can help them direct their future and protect their language and culture.

Indian Rights Confirmed

The James Bay case made aboriginal rights the centre of media and public attention. But it was the case of the Nishga Indians of British Columbia, also heard in 1973, that brought the whole issue of native claims into focus.

The province of British Columbia had consistently denied the existence of an aboriginal interest in the land. After many years of persistence, the Nishga succeeded in bringing their fight for recognition of aboriginal title to the Supreme Court of Canada. The issue at stake was whether or not such title existed in law.

Although dismissing the case on a technicality, the judges split three-three on whether native title still applied or had been extinguished. A review of this decision in August 1973 led the federal government to announce its willingness to negotiate land claims based on outstanding aboriginal title.

The government's objective in settling these land claims was to exchange undefined aboriginal rights for concrete rights and benefits in law.

Native Claims

The 1973 government policy statement acknowledged two broad classes of claims, comprehensive and specific.

Comprehensive claims are based on traditional native use and occupancy of land. Such claims arise in those parts of Canada where the native title has not previously been dealt with by treaty or other means. These areas include Yukon, Labrador, most of British Columbia, northern Quebec and the Northwest Territories. The claims are termed "comprehensive" because of their wide scope. Comprehensive claims encompass such elements as land title, fishing and trapping rights, financial compensation and other economic and social benefits.

Specific claims, on the other hand, deal with specific grievances that Indians may have regarding the fulfilment of treaties. Specific claims also cover grievances arising out of the administration of Indian lands and other assets under the Indian Act.

From the early 1970s to the end of March 1985, the government provided native groups with approximately $87.7 million in loans and $36.7 million in accountable contributions. This money has enabled the Indian people to conduct research into treaties and aboriginal rights and to research, develop and negotiate their claims.

In 1974 the government also established an office within the Department of Indian Affairs and Northern Development to coordinate the assessment of claims from native groups and represent the department and the federal government in negotiations with groups whose claims would be accepted by the minister.

In 1981 the government announced an expansion of its 1973 policy on comprehensive claims and reaffirmed its commitment to negotiate claims of this type. The policy was expanded as a result of the many developments since 1973, and because of the concerns expressed over the years by native groups.

A similar review of the policy on specific claims was conducted in 1981-82. The resulting policy, announced in 1982, reaffirmed and strengthened the government's commitment to meet its lawful obligations to Indian people. It also broadened the basis of acceptance of claims and substantially increased funding to Indian associations for claims research.

Comprehensive Claims

At the end of 1985, in the area of comprehensive claims negotiations were under way with the Dene and Metis of the Mackenzie Valley, the Nishga of northwestern British Columbia and the Conseil Attikamek-Montagnais (CAM) of Quebec. The Council for Yukon Indians claim was undergoing reassessment by both parties.

As of the autumn 1985, there were an additional 15 comprehensive claims awaiting negotiation, seven under review and a further 13 anticipated.

The status of the comprehensive claims then under negotiation is described in the following outline.

Council for Yukon Indians (CYI)

Yukon Indian bands submitted a formal proposal for a claims settlement in 1973. At the end of 1985, the Council for Yukon Indians was negotiating its claim on behalf of both status and non-status Indians of the Yukon Territory.

Claiming traditional use and occupancy of nearly all Yukon, the CYI was asking for outright ownership of lands for native communities. The proposal called for exclusive hunting, fishing and trapping rights over other lands, as well as cash compensation for the loss and past use of Indian land. The Council for Yukon Indians was also seeking a share in resource development.

Early in 1984 an overall agreement in principle was reached by negotiators representing the CYI, the Yukon territorial government and the federal government. That agreement in principle was, however, not ratified by CYI membership. Yukon bands presented the government with various options for resuming negotiations.

The Dene Nation and the Metis Association of the Northwest Territories

In 1976 and 1977 respectively the Dene and Metis organizations of the Northwest Territories presented their claims on behalf of the descendants of the native people who were living in the Mackenzie Valley at the time Treaty Nos. 8 and 11 were signed. The government agreed to accept these claims because not all the treaty provisions had been fulfilled. The negotiations were conducted by a joint Land Claims Secretariat established by the Dene Nation and the Metis Association of the Northwest Territories in 1983.

The two groups claim aboriginal use and occupancy of approximately 1 165 000 square kilometres of land. Issues like ownership of land, native harvesting rights and access to resources are all included in the claim. In addition, the Dene want political control over their claim area.

The Conseil Attikamek-Montagnais (CAM)

The Conseil Attikamek-Montagnais (CAM) represents Indian claimants on the north shore of the St. Lawrence River and the Saguenay and Mauricie areas of Quebec. CAM's claim was accepted for negotiation by the federal government in 1979 and by the Quebec government in 1980. The claim concerns land in the "Indian Corridor" between the northern boundary established by the 1763 Royal Proclamation and the southern boundary of the James Bay territory. The Montagnais have also claimed certain interests in the James Bay territory and in Labrador.

Formal tripartite negotiations began in April 1983, and agreement was reached on the negotiation process to be followed. In November 1984 CAM submitted a proposal on a wildlife and management regime.

The Nishga Tribal Council

In 1976 the Nishga Tribal Council submitted to the federal government and the province of British Columbia a land claim asserting aboriginal title to approximately 14 760 square kilometres of the Nass River Valley. Full provincial participation in the tripartite negotiations was affected by two items: the province's preference for a federal-provincial agreement as a prerequisite to negotiations, and provincial concern about the Nishga position on aboriginal title.

At the end of 1985, however, the federal and provincial governments were continuing to seek a co-operative approach to resolving these items. In addition, progress in negotiations has been made on the fisheries component of the Nishga claim relating to fleet management and resource management.

Specific Claims

Since 1970, more than 280 specific claims have been submitted to the federal government. By the end of 1985, 45 of these claims had been settled. Only 21 claims — a relatively small proportion — were rejected. Sixty-five claims were under negotiation and another 79 were under review.

The specific claims currently being reviewed range from long-standing grievances about loss of reserve lands to allegations of fraud on the part of officials in the past. Alleged failure to fulfil treaty obligations is another specific claims grievance.

The case of the British Columbia "cut-off lands" exemplifies the kind of grievance raised in the specific claims area. In this claim, 22 British Columbia bands contended that some 13 500 hectares of land were cut off their reserves in violation of a promise that the consent of Indian bands would be sought.

In 1975 both the federal and provincial governments decided to negotiate a settlement with these bands. As of March 1985, eight of these claims had been settled.

Yet another example of a specific claims settlement is that of the Wagmatook Band of Nova Scotia. In 1982 the band received $1.2 million in exchange for lands removed from its reserve almost a century ago. This settlement will enable the band to purchase land on the open market and to undertake business ventures.

Economic Development

Whether through claims settlements or other means, Indian people see community-based economic development as the key element in their future self-determination. To date, many viable businesses have been established in Indian communities across the country.

Some of these businesses have been aided by the Indian Economic Development Fund established in the 1970s by the Department of Indian Affairs and Northern Development. Investment has been made in a wide variety of businesses, including motels, tourist resorts, craft industries, grain farming and canoe manufacturing.

Several of these projects are devoted to preserving Indian culture, language and way of life. The Stoney Indians of Morley, Alberta, for example, borrowed from the Indian Economic Development Fund to create the Stoney Wilderness Centre. The centre's purpose is to teach non-native people about the Stoneys' culture, philosophy and religion. Campers enrolled in the program live in tipis on the reserve and are taught survival skills and ancient legends.

Other sources of economic opportunity for Indian people are the major resource development projects undertaken in the vicinity of reserves. In northwest Alberta the Dene Tha Band developed a construction company to meet the needs of the Norman Wells oil field expansion and pipeline project. In northern Ontario the Indian organization, Grand Council Treaty No. 9, successfully negotiated with a local mine for jobs and transportation to and from the work site.

A different type of opportunity arose for the Lax Kw'alaams band of Port Simpson, British Columbia. In October 1984 the band concluded an agreement with Dome Petroleum Limited. The agreement centres on Dome's proposal to build a liquefied natural gas plant at a cost of about $1.7 million. The plant would be situated about three kilometres from the band's home reserve. If the project goes ahead, the band will receive several million dollars' worth of benefits. These will include revenue from sales, employment and training for band members and improvement of nearby salmon streams. Before deciding whether to accept the project, the band commissioned independent studies to assess potential socio-economic and environmental impact.

Historic Breakthroughs of the 1980s

Several remarkable events in the 1980s have brought Indian people closer than ever before to their long-held goal of self-determination within Canadian society. Each of these events owes much to the persistent efforts of Indian people themselves, particularly over the last four decades.

The first of these events was the recognition in the 1982 Constitution Act of the existing aboriginal and treaty rights of the Indian, Inuit and Metis people of Canada. Native leaders played a vigorous role in the negotiations leading up to the passage of the Constitution Act, by which Canada obtained for the first time a formal constitution approved by the Canadian Parliament.

The second historic breakthrough for Indian people was the First Ministers' Conference on Aboriginal Constitutional Matters held in March 1983. The federal government, representatives of Yukon, the Northwest Territories and nine provincial governments, along with aboriginal leaders from across Canada, signed an accord to amend the country's constitution. These four amendments included constitutional recognition of rights acquired through land claims agreements, the guarantee of aboriginal and treaty rights equally to men and women, the commitment to consult aboriginal peoples before any changes affecting them were enacted, and provision for a continuing series of conferences on aboriginal matters into 1987.

At conferences held in 1984 and 1985, aboriginal leaders and first ministers pursued discussions on aboriginal title and aboriginal rights, land and resources and self-government.

The Special Committee on Indian Self-government

The 1983 report of the Special Committee on Indian Self-government had a resounding impact on Indian people and government.

Parliament created the special committee in December 1982 because of shortcomings in the administration of the Indian Act and continued demands by Indian people for more power and an improved standard of life.

The committee received its information in three ways: from oral testimony at public meetings where committee members questioned witnesses, from submissions made in writing, and from research projects it had commissioned. The committee tried to hear as many oral presentations as possible. Criteria were established for selecting witnesses to ensure a representative cross-section of Indian bands and organizations. In total, the committee members heard 567 witnesses during 215 presentations at 60 public meetings across the country.

In its reports, the committee emphasized the value of the understanding it had gained during the hearings. All Canadians, it said, would benefit from similar information so that their understanding of their relationship to Indian First Nations could be extended. They would then learn that "Indians were peoples who moved from free, self-sustaining First Nations to a state of dependency and social disorganization as the result of a hundred years of nearly total government control."

At the beginning of its report, the special committee pinpointed facts indicating the extent of this social disorganization. It noted that despite improvements over the past 10 years, the death rate among Indians remained two to four times the rate for non-Indians. It pointed to the high proportion of Indian children in child care institutions — five times the national rate. It also focused on education statistics — only 20 per cent of Indian children stayed in school to the end of high school, compared to the national rate of 75 per cent.

Yet, as the report stressed, Indian people were faced with an array of bureaucratic and legal obstacles that limit their ability to act on these social conditions. According to Indian witnesses who appeared before the committee, only Indian control of legislation and policy in key areas would ensure the survival and development of Indian communities.

Three areas that Indian witnesses and the committee both considered critical were education, child welfare and health. In particular, witnesses emphasized the need for preventive and holistic health care. To prevent illness, a whole range of living conditions would have to be improved. Better water and sanitation systems would be required. Housing of a standard comparable to that of other Canadians would have to be built. Unemployment, which could lead to alcohol dependency, would have to be ended.

The conclusion of the special committee's report contained 58 recommendations. The first of these was that the federal government should establish a new relationship with the Indian First Nations, and that an essential element of this relationship must be Indian self-government.

The committee also saw control of a strong economic base to be essential for self-government. It recommended that a new relationship between the federal government and Indian First Nations should ultimately provide Indians with an adequate land and resource base, as well as claims settlements. Other recommendations dealt with Indian control of band membership, lands and resources and fiscal arrangements with government.

According to the committee, the prerequisite for the new relationship between the federal government and First Nations was constitutional recognition of Indian rights to self-government. In the meantime, new legislation should make possible the handing over of a wide range of self-government powers to Indian bands, groups of bands or other groupings. Negotiations in each case would decide the exact jurisdiction, which should include authority to legislate in such areas as social and cultural development and justice and law enforcement.

The federal government has confirmed its commitment to Indian self-government and to seeing it entrenched in the constitution. Regular discussions are currently being held about a proposal that would meet the concerns of Indian people, provincial and territorial leaders and the federal government.

Since September 1984, the minister of Indian Affairs and Northern Development has met with as many Indian people as possible to gain an understanding of their perspective on self-government issues. These meetings have revealed anew that the diversity of Indian cultures and traditions will require different forms of self-government across the country.

The Elimination of Sex Discrimination

In June 1985 Parliament passed legislation ending over 100 years of discrimination in the Indian Act. The amendments to the act enabled all Indians who had lost status because of its earlier unfair provisions to have that status restored.

These included Indian women who had lost their status and band membership when they married non-Indians. Another 8 000 Indians who had been voluntarily or involuntarily enfranchised under the act could also have their Indian status restored. Some of them had been enfranchised on joining the clergy, completing university, deciding to vote in federal elections or joining the armed forces.

Indian status was also to be given to the first generation of descendants of those who had unfairly lost their status and band membership.

The amendments also took into account the right of Indian First Nations to control their own membership. In recognition of this right, first-generation descendants of Indians whose status was restored would have to apply to bands themselves for band membership.

Fittingly, the first person in Canada to regain Indian status under the amendments was Mary Two-Axe Early, who had fought against the unjust discrimination in the act since 1968. A Mohawk Indian from the Kaknawake reserve, she had lost her Indian status when she married a non-Indian. For years she had dedicated herself to researching and lobbying on behalf of other women who found themselves in her situation.

Similar dedication and persistence have marked the efforts of Indian leaders and organizations to gain for Indian people their rightful place in Canadian society. The goal is nothing less than a new relationship that respects the diversity, rights and traditions of Indian First Nations.

Directory of Indian and Related Organizations

Indian Associations

Assembly of First Nations
47 Clarence Street
Suite 300, Atrium Building
Ottawa, Ontario K1N 9K1
(613) 236-0673

Prairie Treaty Nations Alliance
(Prairie Regional Council)
11630 Kingsway Avenue
Edmonton, Alberta T5G 0X5
(403) 452-4330

Union of British Columbia Indian Chiefs
440 West Hastings Street
Vancouver, British Columbia
V6B 1L1
(604) 684-0231

Indian Association of Alberta
11630 Kingsway Avenue
Edmonton, Alberta T5G 0X5
(403) 452-4330

Federation of Saskatchewan Indian Nations
1100 1st Avenue East
Prince Albert, Saskatchewan
S6V 2A7
(306) 764-3411

First Nations Confederacy
274 Garry Street
Winnipeg, Manitoba R3C 1H3
(204) 994-8245

Association of Iroquois and Allied Indians
920 Commissioners Road East
London, Ontario N5Z 3J1
(519) 681-3551

Grand Council Treaty No. 3
P.O. Box 1720
Kenora, Ontario P9N 3X7
(807) 548-4215

Union of Ontario Indians
2nd Floor
27 Queen Street East
Toronto, Ontario M5C 1R2
(416) 366-3527

Confederacy of Indians of Quebec
P.O. Box 443
Restigouche, Quebec G0C 2R0
(418) 788-5336

Conseil Attikamek-Montagnais
80 Boulevard Bastien
Village des Hurons
Lorette, Quebec G0A 4V0
(418) 842-0277

Grand Council of the Crees
1500 Sullivan Road
Val d'Or, Quebec J9P 1M1
(819) 825-3402

Union of New Brunswick Indians
35 Dedam Street
Fredericton, New Brunswick
E3A 2V2
(506) 472-6281

Union of Nova Scotia Indians
P.O. Box 961
Sydney, Nova Scotia B1P 6J4
(902) 539-4107

Dene Nation
P.O. Box 2338
Yellowknife, Northwest Territories
X1A 2P7
(403) 873-4081

Council for Yukon Indians
22 Nisutlin Drive
Whitehorse, Yukon Territory
Y1A 2S5
(403) 667-7631

National Indian Arts and Crafts
Corporation
141 Laurier Avenue West
Suite 604
Ottawa, Ontario K1P 5J3
(613) 232-3436

Native Associations

Native Council of Canada
450 Rideau street
4th Floor
Ottawa, Ontario K1N 5Z4
(613) 238-3511

Metis Association of the Northwest
Territories
P.O. Box 1375
Yellowknife, Northwest Territories
X0E 1H0
(403) 873-3505

United Native Nations
1682 West 7th Avenue, Suite 300
Vancouver, British Columbia
V6J 4S6
(604) 732-1201

Native Women's Association of
Canada
195-A Bank Street
Ottawa, Ontario K2P 1W7
(613) 236-6057

Selected Reading

Traditional Cultures

Assiniwi, Bernard. *Indian Recipes.* Toronto: Copp Clark, 1972.

Densmore, Frances. *Chippewa Customs.* Minneapolis: Ross and Haines Inc., 1970.

Densmore, Frances. *How Indians Used Wild Plants for Food, Medicine and Crafts.* New York: Dover Publications, 1974.

Driver, Harold. *Indians of North America.* Chicago: University of Chicago Press, 1967.

Drucker, Philip. *Indians of the Northwest Coast.* New York: American Museum Science Books, 1963.

Hodge, Frederick W., ed., *Handbook of the Indians of Canada.* New York: Krauss Reprint Co., 1969.

Jenness, Diamond. *Indians of Canada.* Ottawa: Queen's Printer, 1955.

Laubin, Reginald and Gladys. *The Indian Tipi.* Norman: University of Oklahoma, 1984.

National Museum of Man. *The Athapaskans: Strangers of the North.* Ottawa: National Museums of Canada, 1974.

Smithsonian Institution. *Handbook of the North American Indians, Vol. 6: Subarctic.* Washington: Smithsonian Institution, 1981.

Smithsonian Institution. *Handbook of the North American Indian, Vol. 15: Northeast.* Washington: Smithsonian Institution, 1978.

Speck, Frank G., *The Iroquois.* Cranbrook Institute of Science, Bulletin 23. Michigan: Cranbrook Press, 1971.

Trigger, Bruce G. *The Children of Aataentsic: A History of the Huron People to 1600.* Vols. 1 and 2. Montreal and London: McGill-Queen's University Press, 1974.

Woodcock, George. *Peoples of the Coast.* Edmonton: Hurtig, 1977.

History (1500 to present)

Brody, Hugh. *Maps and Dreams: Indians and the British Columbia Frontier.* Vancouver: Douglas and McIntyre, 1981.

Crowe, Keith. *A History of the Original Peoples of Northern Canada.* Montreal: McGill-Queen's University Press, 1974.

Innis, H.A., *The Fur Trade in Canada.* Toronto: University of Toronto Press, 1976.

Martin, Calvin. *Keepers of the Game: Indian-Animal Relationships and the Fur Trade.* Berkeley: University of California Press, 1978.

Patterson, E. Palmer. *The Canadian Indian: A History Since 1500.* Toronto: Collier-MacMillan Canada, 1972.

Richardson, Boyce. *Strangers Devour the Land. A Chronicle of the Assault Upon the Last Coherent Hunting Culture in North America, the Cree Indians of Quebec.* Toronto: MacMillan of Canada, 1976.

Sealey, D. Bruce and Lussier, Antoine S. *The Metis: Canada's Forgotten People.* Winnipeg: Manitoba Metis Federation Press, 1975.

Government Publications

Brown, G. and Maguire, R. *Indian Treaties in Historical Perspective.* Ottawa: Department of Indian Affairs and Northern Development (DIAND), 1979.

A Catalogue of Statistical Data in the Program Reference Centre. Ottawa: DIAND, 1983.

Changes in the Indian Act. Ottawa: DIAND, 1985.

(Claims) Fact Sheets. Ottawa: DIAND, 1985.

Comprehensive Claims Map. Ottawa: DIAND.

Contemporary Indian and Inuit Art of Canada. Ottawa: DIAND, 1983.

Historical Development of the Indian Act. Ottawa: Treaties and Historical Research Centre, DIAND, 1981.

Research Reports 1984. Research Branch, DIAND, 1984.

Specific Claims in Canada: Status Report. Ottawa, DIAND, 1984.